Global Journalism

Simon Cottle
General Editor

Vol. 11

The Global Crises and the Media series is part
of the Peter Lang Media and Communication list.
Every volume is peer reviewed and meets
the highest quality standards for content and production.

PETER LANG
New York • Washington, D.C./Baltimore • Bern
Frankfurt • Berlin • Brussels • Vienna • Oxford

Peter Berglez

Global Journalism

Theory and Practice

PETER LANG
New York • Washington, D.C./Baltimore • Bern
Frankfurt • Berlin • Brussels • Vienna • Oxford

Library of Congress Cataloging-in-Publication Data
Berglez, Peter.
Global journalism: theory and practice / Peter Berglez.
pages cm — (Global crises and the media; vol. 11)
Includes bibliographical references and index.
1. Journalism. 2. Online journalism. I. Title.
PN4775.B444   070.4—dc23   2013007659
ISBN 978-1-4331-1031-3 (hardcover)
ISBN 978-1-4331-1030-6 (paperback)
ISBN 978-1-4539-1088-7 (e-book)
ISSN 1947-2587

Bibliographic information published by **Die Deutsche Nationalbibliothek**.
Die Deutsche Nationalbibliothek lists this publication in the "Deutsche
Nationalbibliografie"; detailed bibliographic data is available
on the Internet at http://dnb.d-nb.de/.

© 2013 Peter Lang Publishing, Inc., New York
29 Broadway, 18th floor, New York, NY 10006
www.peterlang.com

All rights reserved.
Reprint or reproduction, even partially, in all forms such as microfilm,
xerography, microfiche, microcard, and offset strictly prohibited.

*Journalism used to be about gathering information and presenting it.
Now everybody does that, so journalism must change
(Tweet from Smarimc, January 14, 2012).*

Contents

Tables and Figures ix

Series Editor's Preface xi

Preface xv

Acknowledgments xix

1. Global Journalism: An Introduction 1

2. So What Exactly Is Global Journalism? 21

3. The Relevance of Global Journalism 51

4. Challenges to Global Journalism 79

5. Global Journalism and the Digital Web 105

Epilogue 125

Notes 131

References 137

Index 153

Tables and Figures

Table 2.1
The Difference Between a Global and Cosmopolitan Outlook 26

Table 2.2
Space, Power, and Identity in Global Journalism 35

Table 2.3
Global Crises and Issues in the News 44

Table 2.4
Various Combinations of Global Journalism in the News 48

Table 3.1
The Basic Difference Between News "in" the Global Village
and News "for" the Global Village 60

Table 3.2
News and Journalism in the Westphalian and Post-Westphalian
Orders from a Global Journalistic Viewpoint 66

Table 3.3
The Two Main Types of Global Journalism and Their Characteristics 69

Table 4.1
Various Challenges to Global Journalism 80

Table 4.2
The Cognitive and Discursive Handling of
the Proximate and Distant in Global Journalism 86

Table 5.1
Global Journalism on the Web from Three Perspectives 121

Figure 5.1
Global Journalism on the Web 114

Figure 5.2
The Hypertextual Organization of Global Causes 118

Figure 5.3
Globalizing News Discourse on the Web 122

Series Editor's Preface

Global Crises and the Media

We live in a global age. We inhabit a world that has become radically interconnected, interdependent, and communicated in the formations and flows of the media. This same world also spawns proliferating, often interpenetrating, "global crises."

From climate change to the war on terror, financial meltdowns to forced migrations, pandemics to world poverty, and humanitarian disasters to the denial of human rights, these and other crises represent the dark side of our globalized planet. Their origins and outcomes are not confined behind national borders and they are not best conceived through national prisms of understanding. The impacts of global crises often register across "sovereign" national territories, surrounding regions and beyond, and they can also become subject to systems of governance and forms of civil society response that are no less encompassing or transnational in scope. In today's interdependent world, global crises cannot be regarded as exceptional or aberrant events only, erupting without rhyme or reason or dislocated from the contemporary world (dis)order. They are endemic to the contemporary global world, deeply enmeshed within it. And so too are they highly dependent on the world's media and communication networks.

The series *Global Crises and the Media* sets out to examine not only the media's role in the *communication* of global threats and crises but also how they can variously enter into their *constitution,* enacting them on the public stage and helping to shape their future trajectory around the world. More specifically, the volumes in this series seek to: (1) contextualize the study of global crisis reporting in relation to wider debates about the changing flows and formations of world media communication; (2) address how global crises become variously communicated and contested in both so-called "old" and "new" media around the world; (3) consider the possible impacts of global crisis reporting on public awareness, political action, and policy responses; (4) showcase the very latest research findings and discussion from leading authorities in their respective fields of inquiry; and (5) contribute to the development of positions of theory and debate that deliberately move beyond national parochialisms and/or geographically disaggregated research agendas. In these ways the specially commissioned books in the *Global Crises and the Media* series aim to provide a sophisticated and empirically engaged understanding of the media's changing roles in global crises and thereby contribute to academic and public debate about some of the most significant global threats, conflicts, and contentions in the world today.

Every now and then a book comes along that stands head and shoulders above the rest. Such books interrupt as much as intervene within extant fields of scholarship. They invite us to revisit, re-conceptualize and re-theorize our views on and approaches to the study of a particular subject domain or substantive range of problems. Such invitations to *re-think* established ways of conceiving and knowing are generally to be welcomed; they can help to extend the parameters of a subject field or, sometimes, completely redefine it and re-orient research. In an earlier time when "normal" and "routine" study in established fields of academic inquiry was perhaps not in quite the current state of multi-disciplinary and interdisciplinary flux and epistemological profusion that it is now, such interventions may have been seen in terms of "paradigm shift." Peter Berglez's *Global Journalism: Theory and Practice* is one of those rare, special books that can help to steer the field of scholarship into a new and necessary trajectory. His book specially commissioned for the *Global Crises and Media Series* does more than simply explore the changing nature of journalism in a global context; it asks us to seriously consider and radically reconceive what global journalism is and can yet become in a globalized world.

Global Journalism: Theory and Practice tackles head on the conceptual *myopia* and underdevelopment of theory in the contemporary field of thinking about "the global journalist" and "global journalism". In an increasingly globalized age of interconnection, interdependency and shared threats it is time to question and challenge the conceptualization of "the global" as simply the sum of national parts, including ideas of "global journalism" conceived as the collection of national journalisms or journalist cultures found around the world. The flows and formations of journalism, we know, increasingly extend beyond national frontiers and interpenetrate within today's complex world news ecology. The professional frontiers of journalism are themselves becoming increasingly porous with the rise of new social media and citizen journalists who now inject a flood of images and ideas from afar, sometimes into mainstream news agendas and/or bypassing traditional news gatekeepers all together.

This new ferment in the field requires that we map and explore not only journalism's demographics and commitments to professional norms and values within particular national contexts, but also how journalism horizons may now also be on the move, infused by, but also contributing to, a more globalized awareness and outlook on events, processes and issues in the world today. What are the journalist practices and dispositions today that exist both inside as well as outside of nationally conceived journalism formations that could yet serve to address or deepen our understanding of our global age? To what extent and how do journalists help us to make sense of those breaking and routine news stories that speak to an interdependent and impacting world of interests and identities? How can and how should "global journalists" help to recover and illuminate the complex interconnections and inequalities, causations and human consequences of living in a globalized world?

Peter Berglez's intervention is unquestionably cutting-edge and seminal. Its importance, moreover, is not confined to the academic fields of journalism studies or even media and communication studies more widely, but speaks to what it now means—politically, socially and culturally—to live within a globalized world and the responsibilities that this places upon us all, including today's journalists. Global journalism, Berglez argued in an earlier article and which here becomes richly elaborated, "is the form of journalism needed in times of globalization" (2008: 855). Global journalism does not, therefore, simply imply extensive geographical or global reach, but depends rather on the extent to which news, whether about local, national, international or transnational events and developments, becomes properly situated and explained in terms of wider and reciprocally interacting global social relations and contours of power. This is a necessary departure from the national or even nationally comparative focus of much contemporary journalism scholarship today, and it is one that scholars undoubtedly will need to take on board, develop and apply in the years ahead. Berglez's theoretical disquisition on global journalism as well as his formulation of analytically incisive concepts with which to interrogate it, provides not only a rich theoretical platform for further work in this area but also a methodological tool-box of enormous practical utility for scholars and students who will follow in his footsteps. This is an important and original book and it is one that demands to be read by all of us who are concerned by the dark side of globalization, its inequalities and injustices, and who see an emergent journalism as performing a crucial role in its democratization and humanization.

—Simon Cottle, Series Editor

Preface

In this volume, my intention is to *theoretically* develop the concept of global journalism and to present analyses of its practice, that is, the kind of reporting that makes the "global village" present in the everyday news, especially in the local newspaper or the national news. I hope that this book will be relevant in the field of global journalism studies and international communication and useful to media and journalism scholars, students, journalism educators, media practitioners as well as to others interested in the present state and future of news journalism. The psychoanalytical background to this study consists of my childhood in a small country in southwest Sweden in the 1980s and my mediated experiences of the Cold War and the Chernobyl disaster in 1986, which also affected my country. Like many other children at this time, I had a bout of nuclear anxiety and sleepless nights: What if the world's leaders would—consciously or by mistake—press the red button? As a consequence, I began to think about the world outside Sweden more than before—the size of it; how to conceive presence and distance; borders, and interconnections between different parts of the globe.

Since then, many events and processes have taken place that affected the whole world, including 9/11, at least one serious financial meltdown, and the emergence of the Internet and WWW. And thanks to climate science, we have become even more aware of the negative effects of our CO_2 emissions (global warming). To this list, we could add the myriads of less visible cross-continental relations between nation-states which media seldom capture, for example, how our micro-oriented everyday behaviors constantly influence peoples' micro-oriented everyday lives in other countries. I am aware that, as a researcher, it's my job and duty to constantly uphold a critical and skeptical stance toward all kinds of ideas, theories, and hypotheses, including my own. But some things are crystal clear to me. For example, that news media (in general) shut out our "global realities" too often in everyday reporting. Personally, I want more of these realities, and I think it would be a good thing for society if this would become realized as soon as possible. This view is based on my own perception of the news media, but I know that I share this opinion with many other media scholars—as will be evident in this book—as well as with many media practitioners and, of course, many news consumers around the world. A fundamental aspect of "modern subjectivity" has driven me to write this book: my inability to accept the fact that some of society's institutions do not develop quickly enough. Although some institutions and practices are able to quickly adapt to new conditions, and/or steer the future development, some lag behind to the extent that they begin to actively *resist* what is happening in society. When it comes to adapting to a globalizing social reality characterized by cross-continental interconnections and common global problems, news media in general have proven to be rather sluggish. News journalism is not in sync with the globalizing development of society. Or to put it in this way: *it is not there yet*. One should think of global journalism as something other than occasional news reports on world terrorism and climate change; think of it as something more *pervasive*. I am aware that it might seem strange to claim that mainstream "news" is one of the conservative institutions in society, as this is not the way news media are primarily perceived. The Catholic Church might, in several respects, be viewed as very conservative, but the daily news? Of course, I will clarify my point on this important matter throughout the book.

Global journalism is probably associated with "corrective" forms of journalism—peace journalism, development journalism, public journalism, human rights journalism, or alternative journalism. Peace journalism, for example, poses very relevant questions about the taken-for-granted basics of mainstream news production and media logic and moves to change some of those discursive fundaments, such as the journalistic tendency to frame reality in terms of conflicts between parties instead of actively promoting peace and understanding. Thus, this critique, as well as other critiques emanating from "corrective" forms of journalism, comes from *outside* of regular media logic, of how "normal" news media tend to work. An important point of this book is that, even if global journalism is, in several respects, based on a questioning of "normal" news journalism, it is not "corrective" in the same sense. Global journalism should emerge from the *inside* of existing mainstream news journalism. It does not arrive from some distant ethical, cultural, discursive, or political planet but from "within" the fundamentals of modern news journalism. Somewhat analogous to what this book will refer to as the present post-Westphalian order (of ever more interdependent nation-states), global journalism should be seen as the natural next step for, and necessary updating of, contemporary news journalism.

Certainly, in arguing for the paramount importance of an expansion of a somewhat new type of reporting called "global journalism" given the critical economic problems of the news media business, one runs the risk of being labeled a "utopianist" and accused of cultivating an academic and theoretical fantasy. At the end of the day, in this book, perhaps I will appear to be another utopian realist of the sort that the Slovenian philosopher Slavoj Žižek writes about who cries: "Let us be Realists and Demand the Impossible!" The tough but still inspiring task is to demonstrate that those of us who argue for more global journalism in the news are actually the only realists in town. Consequently, the true utopians are those who believe that news journalism could stay the same forever.

—Örebro, Sweden, November 30, 2012

Acknowledgments

First of all, I wish to express my gratitude and thanks to Simon Cottle for his support and valuable critique of the chapter drafts throughout the process. I am very grateful that Simon, as the editor of the book series *Global Crises and the Media*, and Peter Lang Publishing gave me the opportunity to fulfill this project. I would also like to thank Mary Savigar, Senior Acquisitions Editor at Peter Lang, and Sophie Appel, Design and Production Supervisor at Peter Lang, for the encouraging and supportive communication across the Atlantic.

I would like to thank the Swedish news company Aftonbladet, and the National Labor Committee for permitting me to reprint some of their images and graphical presentations in this book.

Much thanks to the Research School of Democracy (FDV) and the Media and Communications Department (MKV) at the HumES Department, Örebro University, which provided me with intellectually stimulating research environments and pleasant companionship during the writing process. Thanks also to the masters' students of our programs, Global Journalism and Journalism Connected, who shared their relevant viewpoints on global journalism during lectures and seminars.

My gratitude goes to Johan Östman and Leonor Camauër who contributed with important suggestions on how to improve chapter 4, as well as to Ansgard Heinrich who reviewed chapter 5. However, I am responsible for all the flaws and shortcomings which might occur in the book. I would also like to thank my research colleague, Ulrika Olausson, for contributing important ideas on the relation between globalization, media, culture, and journalism.

Most of all, I would like to thank my wife Tove, and my son Tage, for all the support, sacrifice, and patience throughout the entire process. I dedicate this piece of work to you.

1.

Global Journalism

An Introduction

This book is devoted to global journalism. Its purpose is to contribute to the theoretical development of the very idea of global journalism as well as to analyze its present practice. Two points are stressed and concretely illustrated in the book. First, we need to see global journalism as part of a needed paradigmatic change in the history of news; that news media will have to become much more globally oriented in their everyday reporting than is the case today in order to survive as the institution we have known for the last 200 years, that is, as an important producer of, and/or hub for, democratically and socially relevant information and communication. Second, research, but also journalism education, must become more actively engaged in the epistemological development and refinement of global journalism as a practice; both need to intellectually engage in its particular reporting niches as well as its potential to take online news reporting to the next level. In this first chapter, I will present a basic definition of global journalism and clarify the book's particular approach in relation to the research field as a whole. At the end of the chapter, the entire book's content is introduced in brief summaries of the material covered in each chapter.

GLOBAL JOURNALISM AS THEORY AND PRACTICE

A few years ago, I interviewed journalists in Sweden about their climate reporting (Berglez 2011a; Berglez et al. 2009). What particularly interested me were their reflections on the everyday barriers to presenting news containing a global dimension (such as the global warming); how they found the traditional, and rather strict, division between domestic and foreign worlds/news sections more or less superfluous in an ever-globalizing world, suffering from problems such as climate change. Here, what interested me most was that they were trying to dissociate themselves from the taken-for-granted news practice of clearly separating the domestic from the foreign. More precisely, these journalists were eager to *combine* domestic and foreign climate perspectives in one and the same news story. Gradually, I realized that they were talking about something that I had been looking for quite a while but only found in theory: global journalism—the kind of reporting which manages to make global processes visible and tangible.

My interview research in 2007 proved useful in my attempts to further empirically identify and theoretically crystallize the practice of global journalism. My idea is that global journalism is mainly based on *global outlooks*. I consider the global outlook as a cognitive framework as well as a particular kind of discursive content. Journalists and editors generate such outlooks when demonstrating how society is embedded in global processes, that is, when cognitively and discursively conjuring up a globalizing society. Global journalism usually involves news coverage of global crises such as the "global war on terror," climate change, and financial meltdowns (Cottle 2009a, 2011), or potential ones, for example, nuclear anxiety and emerging pandemics. Furthermore, it includes journalism which contributes to global outlooks on various issues such as consumption, terrorism, crime, energy and agriculture. It is thus possible to see it as a particular mode of reporting or news style/narrating (Berglez 2011b) which "makes it into an everyday routine to investigate how people and their actions, practices, problems, life conditions etc. in different parts of the world are interrelated" (Berglez 2007: 151). I have formulated what I find to be the "essence" of global journalism practice in the form of the following question:

> In what ways and to what extent does news journalism shed light on the interconnectedness of social reality? Is the particular news event narrowly defined as a domestic (local/regional/national) matter (a terror act in Madrid, an HIV catastrophe in Southern Africa etc.), solely explained by domestic factors, or is the journalist also bringing in transnational and global aspects? (Berglez 2008: 849)

However, global journalism is not merely practice, it is theory, too, i.e., developed ideas on what global journalism is and what it ought to be. From a research point of view, focus on the practice of global journalism paves the way for (a) the formulation of theory as to what global journalism might be in a news industry context—as a potential professional identity, newsroom routine, and "genre" along with other kinds of established news forms as well as (b) theory about global journalism's role in society, politically and democratically speaking. To concentrate on both theory and practice, or more precisely, the *theory of the practice of global journalism*, leads to a relatively complete, albeit not absolute, understanding of what its mode of reporting de facto is and might become in the future. Here, the aim is to constantly oscillate between the "facts" (this is what global journalism empirically looks like today) and certain "norms" (this is the way global journalism could or should develop in the future in relation to certain commercial, democratic, or political values). Here, I will apply a relatively wide range of media, journalism, and social theory as well as relevant empirical research.

GLOBALIZATION IS EVERYWHERE BUT WHAT ABOUT GLOBAL JOURNALISM?

To begin with, global journalism is relevant only in relation to the assumed existence of globalization. Whether you live in Zimbabwe, Cincinnati, South East Nicaragua, or St. Petersburg, Russia, globalization is more or less part of society. It is not dominating our everyday lives but it is an important aspect of them. It is characterized by material and discursive cross-continental processes, involving disparate phenomena such as the swine flu AH_1N_1 (a global epidemic), the Internet (a global network) and Kim Kardashian (a global celebrity); it is a social process involving complex relations between peoples as well as a concept with which reality is interpreted and categorized in a particular way (Berglez 2006; Rosenberg 2000). Some stress that globalization is synonymous with market capitalism and its (global) interests (cf. de Sousa 2006) or as a buzzword assumedly invented by Western businesspeople and other elites. However, more balanced definitions usually describe globalization as:

> ...a stretching of social relations and activities across regions and frontiers. ...It suggests a growing magnitude or intensity of global flows such that states and societies become increasingly enmeshed in worldwide systems and networks of interaction. As a consequence, distant occurrences and developments can come to have serious domestic impacts while local happenings can engender significant global repercussions. In other words, globalization represents a significant shift in the spatial reach of social relations and organization towards the interregional or intercontinental scale. This does not mean that the global necessarily displaces or takes precedence over local, national and re-

gional orders of social life. Rather the point is that the local becomes embedded within more expansive sets of interregional relations and networks of power. (Held & McGrew 2003: 3)

However, globalization still tends to appear as a rather elusive and even invisible phenomenon (Fairclough 2006):

> A major feature of the global condition is the wide and glaring hiatus between wealth and poverty. One would like to say it's a feature of global experience, but for how many of us is it a matter of experience? Worlds of experience are segmented and representations across the fence are coded. (Nederveen Pieterse 2000: 129)

> I think that there are representations of globality which have not been recognized as such or are contested representations. Such representations include immigration and its associated cultural environments, often subsumed under the notion of ethnicity. What we still narrate in the language of immigration and ethnicity, I would argue, is actually a series of processes having to do with the globalization of economic activity, of cultural activity, of identity formation. (Sassen 1998: xxxi)

In other words, identified issues such as poverty and immigration seem to be linked with global processes, but what and where *is* "the global" in this context? Perhaps one could understand this in the following way: due to various cross-continental processes, such as environmental pollution, the Internet, industrial production, business, trade, media technology and travel, the world's populations affect each other in more or less obvious ways across continents. However, in exactly these kinds of causal relations and interconnections the global condition tends to "happen" again and again (Jameson 1991: 410–411) and becomes empirically observable. However, in many cases, globalization might seem invisible because it is more or less omnipresent: it is inscribed in the air, the wood, and the buildings; it is in our clothes, the computer, professional language, newspaper, iPhone, employment contract, food basket, car, transportation habits, recycling routines, everyday behavior, working routines, and so forth. As all these objects and practices tend to be intertwined with, or caused by, objects and practices elsewhere, beyond the local or national home territory.

The positive side of globalization is the increasing connectedness and communication between peoples and ideas in the world, while the obvious adverse effects are economic concentration, cultural homogenization, world terrorism, global power interests, the material divide between the Global North and South (Nederveen Pieterse 2000), or that local crises, for example of the environmental or financial sort, might take a global form (Beck 1992, 2010). In other words, globalization generates possibilities, self-fulfillment and connections beyond the local or domestic culture but also social problems, crises, and inequalities. However, perhaps in most cases, ever more globalization should still be seen as the "solution" to global problems, as the only realistic way to politically handle the dark sides of globalization (Cottle 2009a: 22) is through global engagement and exchange. Even an effort to radically "cancel" or repress the globalization for the sake of a "return to the local" around the world would require radical *global* engagement and coordination. In other words, there is really no way back to some pre-global state (Beck 2010).

Media are an important part of globalization, and there is even an established term—media globalization—that refers to the activities and power of (Western) media conglomerates and their global distribution of information and communication goods (Thussu 2006) as well as counter-processes (cf. Curran & Park 2006). It is often pointed out that media and media technology are a central part of globalization, especially in terms of ICTs and the rise of a global network society (Castells 1996). But at the same time, media still tend to be very much "outside" or, rather, exclude themselves from, globalization. At least this is the case when it comes to the generation of news and journalism which includes *globalization as a "reality"* in actual storytelling and coverage of events. Financial and elite-oriented news such as Bloomberg's or Dow Jones's services are globally oriented in their scope and focus, but the news media sector is primarily dominated by media which deliver domestic outlooks—national and/or local viewpoints on politics, social affairs, and democracy (Anderson 1991; Schlesinger 1991; Billig 1995). An old but nevertheless important observation is that media globalization has not generated enough global journalism in the world's mainstream news (Hafez 2007, 2011; Riegert 2011). Generally speaking, there is a deficit of the kind of news discourse which makes us aware of various global processes as such and their complex relations, problems and impacts on all our lives. *There is a global village but it is marginalized in the news,* and this is why global processes so often seem like abstract and distant phenomena instead of "normal" everyday realities. The repression of global realities in everyday mainstream news could be explained by several factors, such as cultural, economic, and ideological ones, but we need to focus more on the way in which this repression is built into the practice and tradition of modern news journalism which has been developing for the past 200 years. The conflict, between, on the one hand, the social material existence of various global processes within our societies, and, on the other hand, the repression of similar processes in mainstream news is then what makes global journalism an urgent research object and an essential challenge for journalism educators, journalists, news companies, and media management.

A SHORT INTRODUCTION TO GLOBAL JOURNALISM RESEARCH

This book's approach needs to be clarified in relation to previous and ongoing global journalism research. Interestingly, there is no common view of what global journalism de facto is, and there is surely no definition that everybody could agree upon. Consequently, global journalism studies have generated rather diverse contributions in which the common denominator seems to be "journalism in the context of globalization" (Reese 2010). In my view, there are three dominant types of global journalism research.

The first type is engaged in globalization and journalism but seldom develops or applies the actual concept of global journalism. See, for example, studies on the political economy of the global media industry (McPhail 1987, 2010; Boyd-Barrett & Rantanen 1998; Sparks 2007; Malek & Kavoori 2000, etc.). This category also includes "global public sphere studies" (Hafez 2007, 2009a, 2009b, 2009c, 2011; Volkmer 1999, 2008; Chitty 2000; Hjarvard 2001a; 2001b) which concentrate on the ways in which transnational networks (CNN International, Al Jazeera, etc.) and/or particular media events (involving wars, conflicts, and catastrophes) generate worldwide media attention and global audiences. In this sort of study, researchers tend to be interested in cultural transformation—that is, how global media affect norms, values, and worldviews—and its ideological consequences (Berglez 2012). They focus on how media and journalism contribute to or become part of media globalization (Thompson 1995), but less attention is paid to whether journalism actively, in concrete reporting, contributes to an understanding of the world as global and/or cross-continental relations. In global media events such as 9/11, the war in Iraq, the tsunami in 2004, and the Arab Spring, a "global consciousness" and the idea that we live in an interconnected world instead might become more or less unintended effects of the actual reporting.

The second type of global journalism research mainly applies to global journalism as a generic concept and concentrates on the universal and particular characteristics of journalism in the world (Deuze 2006). More precisely, it analyzes the potentially universal features of journalism as well as the role of particular journalistic traditions, ideologies, and cultures (Herbert 2003; de Beer & Merrill 2008: Löffelholz & Weaver 2008):

> Global journalism refers to the ongoing evolutionary homogenization of news production structures and standards ("one world") and, at the same time, to the totality of quite distinct journalism cultures representing the different societies of the world. (Löffelholz & Weaver 2008: xiii)

Aspects of this approach can be found in Siebert, Peterson & Schramm's (1956) classic four theories of the press, which were intended to be globally relevant and applicable. In this context, the world's news media were either authoritative (supportive of political power), libertarian (keeping an eye on the government), oriented towards social responsibility (identifying with social concerns), or organized in accordance with the Soviet Communist media model (a propaganda tool). The modernization and de-colonization processes of the 1960s, the NWICO debate of the 70s (see Sosale 2003) as well as crucial political events such as the fall of the Berlin Wall and 9/11 (cf. Tveiten 2006) have paved the way for more complex ways of understanding journalism from a global perspective. New variables have been added, such as the particular political, economic, ethical, religious, technological, and material conditions in various countries and regions of the world (Hallin & Mancini 2004). In this respect, de Beer & Merrill's (2008) widely used anthology, *Global Journalism: Topical Issues and Media Systems*, gathers studies on various journalism cultures from media institutional, technological, commercial, political, ethical, social, and cultural perspectives. Despite the anthology's importance for the global understanding of journalism, its abandonment of the rigid and simplistic model of Siebert, Schramm and Peterson has been criticized from various directions. The main criticism has been its salient Western/American view of journalism and its role for democracy (cf. Josephi 2005) and its disregard of media systems in the world and their complexities (cf. Hallin & Mancini 2004).

Due to the generic use of the concept in both de Beer & Merrill's and Löffelholz & Weaver 's (*Global Journalism Research*) anthologies, global journalism is supposed to represent the complex sum of the world's journalism.[1] As a consequence, global journalism becomes an umbrella concept which is neither very precise nor analytically useful. However, there is a third type of research that considers global journalism as a particular *prac-*

tice, which is also how global journalism is tackled in this book. Here, global journalism is seen as an activity that takes place out in the field or in the editorial office. The focus to date has mainly been on how journalists are supposed to integrate cultural relativism, cosmopolitanism, and non-Western perspectives in news reporting (van Ginneken 2005; Herbert 2003; Seib 2002; Tveiten 2009; Robertson 2010; Wasserman 2010, 2011a), on how to be ethically and culturally reflexive as a journalist in a multicultural and complex world (Ward 2005; 2008). Some studies particularly focus on how journalists and editors participate in the discursive transformation of news media content in a globalizing world (Hamilton & Jenner 2004; Fairclough 2006; Olausson 2011). Reese (2001; 2007; 2008) aims to "theorize a globalized journalism"—to understand the structural change of the profession in times of globalization. Reese seems to be primarily interested in the emergence of a global journalistic guild, equipped with particular values and views on the world, operating in international news environments such as at Reuters and BBC World. The practice of global journalism is defined as "...one that is not necessarily gigantic but carried out in such a way that the producers, users, and subjects need not, and often do not, share a common national orientation" (Reese 2007: 40). That is, global journalism should establish a news environment that goes beyond national orientation in the selection of sources and the actual reporting of events. Another practically oriented research contribution derives from Cottle (2009a; 2009b; 2009c) and his analysis of global crisis reporting, which I consider an important part of the wider practice of global journalism (Cottle 2009a: 42), along with the coverage of global issues (see chapter 2). Cottle's seminal book, *Global Crisis Reporting*, discusses the ways in which, for example, forced migrations, climate change, or "the global war on terror" are handled by journalists. Here, and in other publications, Cottle argues that news coverage of global crises, including natural disasters and humanitarian catastrophes with transnational impacts (Cottle 2011, 2012; Pantti et al. 2012; Yell 2012), has been neglected for too long by media scholars, and more attention needs to be paid to various kinds of impacts (media institutional, political, and democratic). Finally, interesting attempts have recently been made to detect the global journalistic practice in "global imaginary" discourse as identified in the Western news coverage of Barack Obama's speech in Egypt 2008 (Ojala 2011); in the coverage of global climate change summits (Kunelius & Eide 2012) as well as in journalistic representations of an "international community" (Ibold & Ireri 2012).

THE SEARCH FOR "REAL" GLOBAL JOURNALISM AND ITS DISAPPOINTMENTS

Most global journalism scholars, including myself, agree that news journalism with a global outlook is a rather marginalized phenomenon in the general news flow, and that this is a problem. However, there may be different views as to precisely how absent it is in the news. Cottle's and others' (Berglez 2008, 2011a; 2011b plus the above-mentioned studies) recent demonstrations of a possibly emergent global journalism will still not convince all researchers in the field that it actually exists.[2] This empirical disbelief has been voiced by media scholars who would like to see a more globalized journalism (Morris and Waisbord 2001; Roosvall & Moring-Salovaara 2010) but who find few signs of it:

> We do not have much empirical evidence to support the vision of the global village in the sphere of mainstream mass media and classical journalism. (Hafez 2009b: 1)

> There is little evidence that globalization has reshaped the mainstream media's foreign news agendas. International events continue to be framed according to national political, economic, and cultural discourses about the world outside the nation. (Riegert 2009: 133)

> So-called globalization processes seem to be producing more parochial forms of media content. (Phelan & Owen 2010: 27)

There are at least four explanations of the ingrained empirical pessimism. First, in some countries (New Zealand, for example), the lack of news with a global outlook and the traditional foreign news seems to be obvious (Phelan & Owen 2010). The second reason is that often expectations are very high for global journalism, ethically, politically, culturally, and so forth. Some concepts seem to generate very unrealistic projections and dreams of a better world to come, and global journalism is definitively one of them. Some may foster the illusion that global journalism is a bazaar for border-crossing communication as the ultimate multicultural news discourse that could make people all around to become one, and to once and for all establish social equality in the world. Thus, today the practice of global journalism resembles a mission struggling to carry the world's problems on its shoulders. "We must try and understand each other—just like in a real village. Let's improve global journalism!" Hafez states (2009a: 331). It is easy to embrace such words, but as Wasserman

(2010) puts it, there is need for "...a critical global journalism which would be wary of utopian visions of the global" (p. 5). The greater the expectations of a perfect global journalism, the more difficult it becomes to see any empirical signs of it. No matter where one looks, "true" global journalism seems so hard to find.[3] If unrealistic idealism takes over the research agenda, global journalism runs the risk of turning into an unattainable utopian condition instead of a realistic mode of reporting that could be implemented and expanded in various mainstream news.

The third possible explanation of the empirical pessimism is the way global journalism tends to be defined and viewed as a genre (cf. Hamilton and Jenner 2004). For example, Riegert (2009; 2011) seems to argue that global news content could only be produced by transnational networks, such as BBC World, Al Jazeera and CNNi (cf. Volkmer 1999). But no research indicates that, for example, CNNi is producing more global journalism—actively interrelating distant events and processes across continents—than other types of news media, including local ones. Instead most kinds of news media might potentially house global journalism. Reese (2008) is right in claiming that "...a focus only on giant global media firms fails to fully capture the evolving news process" (246). Therefore, we need to become more empirically reflexive and observant on what might discursively evolve in domestic mainstream news, although perhaps in small scale and in the margins. What if some of today's local and national reporters are also global journalists (cf. Hamilton & Jenner 2004)? The spontaneous response to those who question the empirical evidence of global journalism in everyday news should be as follows:

What we look for might be in front of our eyes, we just have to look closer. In fact, global journalism is in your newspaper as well as on the particular news web that caught your attention earlier today. It is present in the story on that company in your own region and its foolhardy investments on the other side of the world; in the critical story on the environment and the entire planet's destiny; in the news documentary on the unforeseen effects of the financial crisis in the US, and in the news of the farmers' worries about global grain prices, which, by the way, appeared in a local news story. It was there in the Mohammad cartoon controversy coverage some years ago, in its interlinking of events and reactions in different parts of the world, and it was present in the coverage of the swine flu crisis—two global crises which proved to be partly invented by the media. Naturally, it is present in the kind of journalism which critically investigates the activities of global companies such as BP or Microsoft, as well as in reports which are tracing the distant and often un-

Global Journalism

known origin of the products we buy. It is present, but marginalized, hidden, or anonymously embedded in traditional news. In any case, it is time to acknowledge and establish its empirical existence in news discourse as well as in media culture.

The fourth reason for pessimism is that some empirical studies that stress the absence of global journalism in mainstream news tend to think of it as traditional international or foreign news (see Altmeppen 2010). As a consequence, they see nothing but a drastic decline, leaning on the fact that news companies around the world tend to cut their costs by closing their foreign offices (Currah 2009). But, as this book will try to demonstrate, the lack of foreign journalism in mainstream news does not necessarily indicate a lack of global journalism, as they are not the same. Foreign journalism concentrates on covering distant events, while global journalism focuses on interrelating distant events across the world as well as on combining domestic and foreign processes. Perhaps one could understand this matter in a Freudian way, assuming that untreated and repressed childhood traumas sooner or later tend to pop up in new forms (in dream work, as sudden anxiety attacks, etc.). In a similar way, traditional foreign news may be systematically repressed for financial reasons, but it is hard to repress it entirely due to globalizing reality's impact on our lives and societies. The "foreign world" instead pops up to the surface in altered news contexts and forms—in climate reporting, agricultural news reports, the domestic news on the "war on terror," and so forth.

BUT IS THIS REALLY SOMETHING NEW?

It is reasonable to assume that global journalism has existed as a practice for a long time, albeit in slightly different disguises and forms. As long as there have been relations between peoples and regions across continents, mediated through trade, cultural exchange, religious antagonism, wars, etc., these transnational relations have been documented, covered and disseminated in various ways, and thereby they have contributed to variants of "global news" (see Rantanen 2009). Roughly speaking, it ought to be possible to imagine Ancient, Persian, Roman, Chinese, medieval, colonial, etc. versions of global journalism. It is also possible to imagine that some historical developments and institutions have paved the way for the rise of contemporary global journalism, such as the birth of international news agencies in the 19th century (see Rantanen 2007, 2009) followed by the rise of global business news. Furthermore, the contemporary modes of global journalism might also be founded on historically important media coverage, such as the coverage of the First and Second World Wars, the Cuban Missile Crisis, the Vietnam War and the 1970s oil crisis. However, what characterizes contemporary global journalism is the more obvious way of interrelating distant events and actions in the world, present in the news coverage of financial meltdowns, ecological disasters, global political affairs, or cross-cultural controversies. Furthermore, even if global journalism might be seen as a "new" phenomenon in mainstream news, it is essential to remember that related modes of communicating have, and still are, flourishing outside news media—in documentaries such as Fredrik Gertten's *Bananas!** (2009); in such films, for example, as Lukas Moodysson's *Mammoth* (2009) and Stephen Gaghan's *Syriana* (2005), or in nonfiction books, including Naomi Klein's (2008) *The Shock Doctrine*.

What has possibly implanted global journalism in contemporary news is the establishment and expansion of the concept of globalization in the social sciences and human society over the past 30 years after the gradual growth of a "globalizing reality" for the last 40–50 years. We have witnessed ever more complex economic, technological, cultural, social, political relations across continents and potential or actual global crises (the nuclear threat or climate change) have been identified and/or constructed by politicians, researchers, opinion makers, governmental institutions or NGOs. Due to the interplay among these developments and mechanisms, a qualitatively new kind of "reality" has become more and more empirically obvious to, and thus co-produced by, news journalism.

TWO NECESSARY AREAS OF DEVELOPMENT

Despite the increasing number of relevant and interesting studies, in my view, global journalism research needs to strengthen and develop two ideas and areas of study in particular.

1. As a normative point of departure, the global journalistic practice should be theorized and analyzed as the "only realistic way" for the kind of news coverage that, also in the future, wants to stay relevant, democratically speaking.

Global journalism's democratic potential primarily lies in its ability to deliver global outlooks and thereby work as a primary introducer of an ever more globalizing reality and society.[4] Its ways of interrelating spatially distant events make news audiences/users increasingly aware of the interconnectedness of today's globalizing society, which in turn, could support various political engagements and struggles within nation-states as well as across national borders. From this perspective, global journalism is not viewed as a representative of one particular journalistic ideal or ethic, as it could possibly interplay with different ideologies—cosmopolitanism, anti-capitalism, ecological thinking, liberalism, Marxism, Christianity, Islam, etc. It might both promote consensus in society and bring conflicts to the surface (cf. Carpentier & Cammaerts 2006) as well as become part of destructive processes such as in much of the 9/11 reporting (Nohrstedt & Ottosen 2004) and the Mohammad cartoon controversy coverage a few years ago (Eide et al. 2008). In other words, it might be exploited by all sorts of interests, including the bad ones (such as political and religious extremists). However, in the "bad" cases, it is hardly global journalism's basic reporting rationale (the interrelating of domestic and foreign events) which could be blamed for the destructive communication but instead, apparent lack of objectivity and the promotion of some particular political agenda or nationalism.

To be more precise, what makes global journalism democratically important is its ability to develop and establish *global political culture* (*glopo culture*). In order to clarify this, we need to look at journalism's role in the reproduction of the modern nation-state. We know that democratic and political deliberation and public engagement within the nation-state very much presuppose institutions such as national media companies and discursive infrastructure in terms of the constant emphasis on, and production of, *national outlooks* on politics and citizenship (Schlesinger 1991; Anderson 1991). Hence, in accordance with the same rationale, long-term goals such as "world cosmopolitanism" or "global democracy"—whatever they might mean—*first of all* require a journalism that increasingly engages in internalizing globalization and global relations in everyday news reporting. This is necessary in order to break the tradition of merely occasional engagement in global politics— usually connected to temporary global crises and particular global media events—and pave the way for the *mainstreaming* of it. Global journalism is a necessary discursive infrastructure for the expansion of a "global consciousness" in political engagement at the, or in relation to, the local (municipal politics), national (parliaments, authorities), regional (EU, AU etc.) and/or global (UN, World Bank etc.) levels of politics (Berglez & Olausson 2011).

Thus, what has not received enough scholarly attention is the idea that mainstream news media's ability to play a democratic role in society increasingly *presupposes* the ability to interconnect the world's continents (i.e., it is not enough to report events from distant countries in accordance with the rationale of foreign correspondence). The survival of broader news media as an important informative and communicative hub and public sphere for the different segments of society (interests, groups, cultures, classes, etc.) will require an expansion of global journalism. Given that globalization and its complex relations continue to develop and expand, global journalism will have to become a normal aspect of all news production. Mainstream news will become residual and hopelessly outdated if it ignores the emergence of a "globalizing society." It will, as Jean Baudrillard (1982/1997) once predicted, gradually become sucked into the black Internet hole of "general information" along with the citizen journalism flow and its multitude of tweets, blogs, and other types of alternative sources with shifting reliability and quality, and which are predominantly endowed with national outlooks on society (Halavais 2000). In the worst case, the products of global journalism will only be consumed by a small and enlightened elite via specialized news, while the "masses" will stick to mainstream media's more "de-global" news (news with predominately domestic content). The continuing lack of global outlooks does not undermine news journalism from a commercial point of view, i.e., it does not make the news less marketable (the traditional, "de-global" kind of news is much easier to sell). However, it definitively undermines its political importance. Therefore, further theoretical work is needed as well as empirical analyses which situate global journalism in a wider media cultural context, focusing on its importance to the future of news journalism's ability to deliver democratically relevant information.

2. When it comes to the required expansion of global journalism in traditional news (including the Web): it is essential to develop the epistemological understanding of its practice in relation to its obvious conflict, but also potential interplay with, traditional news values and routines

There is a continuing lack of studies of the practical side of global journalism, in which the global outlook is perceived as down-to-earth "knowledge production" (Berglez 2007, 2008, 2011b), which concretely "...seeks to understand and explain how economic, political, social and ecological practices, processes and problems in different parts of the world affect each other, are interlocked, or share commonalities" (Berglez 2008: 847). Van Ginneken's (2005) work, *Global News*, discusses the relationship between globalization and news from several relevant perspectives (critical, commercial, cultural, ethical, and discursive) but does not develop the idea of a particular global journalism which actively interconnects different part of the world, not only in terms of intercultural understanding between peoples but also materially, economically, politically, and socially. Reese's (2008) highly important ideas about a "globalizing journalism" are complemented with few empirical demonstrations; i.e., what does it look like in terms of a news coverage, and, more precisely how could it be developed as a mode of reporting? Cottle's (2009a) *Global Crisis Reporting* concentrates on journalism's handling of global crises, but we need to pay attention to the ways in which global crisis reporting paves the way for mainstreaming a global mode of reporting, i.e., its breakthrough and expansion in all kinds of news that might involve global relations. Hence, global crisis reporting is only a part of global journalism but yet an important part.

More precisely, then, there is need for an epistemological approach to global journalism that puts journalists' and news companies' ability to report the world "globally" at the center of analytical attention without letting "classic" media theoretical issues such as objectivity, ethics, critique, or ideology take over the discussion.[5] Not enough attention has been paid to the idea that global journalism also presupposes a *new* kind of reporting competence. From an editorial and media routine point of view, what does it mean, and/or what is required to quickly and smoothly complement the coverage of the South African poaching and illegal animal trade with comments from some European countries and material on similar events/problems in India and China (in order to generate the global outlook)? This process involves the way that fundamental concepts such as space, power, and identity need to be differently dealt with in comparison to traditional local or foreign journalism as well as how the development of global outlooks might collide as well as merge with traditional news values (Berglez 2008, 2011b). This also means particular analytical engagement in already existing, contemporary, examples of global journalistic "techniques" as well as in potential future forms. Only this kind of epistemological approach, which is also rather detailed in practice, could help us to discern whether a globalizing reality actually could become more present in mainstream news media as well as in the context of training. And only in this way can media practitioners and academics discuss global journalism in a meaningful way.

GLOBAL JOURNALISM IS HERE BUT FOR WHOM AND WHY NOW?

The two research approaches to global journalism of course have some barriers to overcome. The following sarcastic comment might be heard either within or outside the domain of research: "What is global journalism if not the awaited consequence of the massive inflation of globalization theory in social research? Nowadays, all kinds of phenomena seem to be defined as global: the economy, the media culture, politics, technology, flows, etc., and finally even journalism.... It is one thing to merge two well-known concepts, global and journalism, but something else entirely to fill it with relevant substance and make it useful for many. So, is there really a need for this concept? What is wrong with the already established ones?"

Global journalism scholars thus need to improve their abilities to fend off this kind of critique and explain why this concept is absolutely necessary for scholars, journalism students and practitioners. Another problem is the continuing dominance of a generic understanding of global journalism as being associated with the entire world's journalism. The possible consequence of this point of view is that global journalism remains a rather imprecise and bland term, which, in turn, represses the essential practical understanding of the term. It must be conceptually treated in the same way as local or foreign journalism. We do not consider local journalism as a generic term because it indicates a rather delimited practice (Franklin 2006), and we need to think about global journalism in the same way.

Global journalism is suffering from an invisibility problem as well. The concept of global journalism is partly established among media and journalism scholars but hardly at all among media practitioners. Few professional journalists would call themselves global journalists. Among most practicing journalists and editors, what is in this book claimed to be empirically observable in the news is nameless or at least not referred to as "global journalism." Nor is the concept widespread among the news audiences/users. Even if various examples of global journalism might quite often pop up on the news Web monitor or in the newspaper, among the news audiences/users, few would define what they watch or read as global journalism but instead as local, foreign, science, health, or world journalism. But "within" these forms or genres, global journalism tends to operate.

However, a concept, i.e., the intellectual aspect of a phenomenon, may come into being retroactively as the effect of a certain practice. Or one might say that global journalism is practiced in various news production contexts despite its weak conceptual status, but the concept might be taking form. In accordance with a similar rationale, the practice of local journalism probably emerged before the very idea of local journalism as a demarcated practice.

And then vice versa. As soon as a concept becomes established and part of the language, it begins to pave the way for certain material and practical developments. In other words, the global journalistic concept's establishment at universities, in media companies, among the public, in education, everyday language, etc. could pave the way for more news that includes global journalism practices. Perhaps sometime in the future, global journalism will become as "normal" as traditional local or foreign journalism. Time will tell.

AN OUTLINE OF THE BOOK

I intend to address the two research challenges discussed above in the following chapters:

Chapter 2. So What Exactly Is Global Journalism?

To begin with, I will examine the practice of global journalism and "confirm" its existence in contemporary news media (more precisely its existence in the margins of the everyday news flow). More precisely, by means of mainstream news media, various examples of global journalistic practices are empirically demonstrated as well as theoretically analyzed, which could be seen as a natural development of my earlier presentations of global journalism (Berglez 2008; 2011). I hope that the chapter could be used in various (journalism) education contexts in order to familiarize students with already existing modes of global reporting and give them a basic sense of contemporary global reporting and storytelling. It is also relevant for those media researchers who intend to empirically analyze global journalism in various media. By examining its basic properties it also becomes easier to understand and suggest how global journalism could be further developed in various directions, such as in the case of the digital Web, which is presented in chapter 5.

Chapter 3. The Relevance of Global Journalism

This chapter is devoted to the relevance of global journalism for the individual (citizen/consumer), the entire society and its various institutions as well as for the future of news journalism as such. Amongst other things, the chapter will give a sociological and historical background to the political and democratic importance of a global outlook in journalism and its obvious conflict with the national outlook in particular, the rather dominant framework in news journalism as we usually know it. In this chapter, another important subject will be the assumed relevance of global outlooks in the coverage of business news and the need to expand this rationale to news production in general, especially in the case of regular domestic (local/national) news.

Chapter 4. Challenges to Global Journalism

This book will stubbornly repeat (again and again) the pivotal importance of expansion as well as further development of global journalism in the general news flow. But, it would be naïve and even wrong to simply ignore all the possible challenges that such a development needs to overcome. Therefore, an entire chapter is devoted to these challenges. Yes, I agree that some of the presented challenges seem more like impenetrable barriers, but the task should be to change the perspective and to show a way out of the tunnel of pessimism and the self-fulfilling prophecy among media practitioners as well as among some journalism scholars and educators that professional news reporting could never change and will always be the same. This includes a suggested way out of global journalism's obvious conflict with the long-established ways of "de-global" (local and national) reporting and news values.

Chapter 5. Global Journalism and the Digital Web

Here, the theory of the practice of global journalism as developed in this book will be applied to online news. Digital media are the natural future of news and journalism, and my primary argument is that (news) Web editors and journalists should strive to take control over the digital technology in terms of using it more creatively in order to develop more advanced ways of covering an ever more complex (global) reality. In order to survive in the long term, professional news journalism should not ignore entirely or simply adjust to various digital technology developments, such as the strong focus on interactivity emanating from the emerging culture of social media. It should seek its own communicative identity on the digital Web, which could pave the way for its rebirth as a professional practice. Here, amongst other professional crossroads, global journalism might serve as one important case. More precisely, the point is to demonstrate the strength and dynamics of hypertextual news reporting, i.e., hyperlinking, in the case of representing the global condition of contemporary society and for the journalistic delivery of advanced global outlooks.

Epilogue

My central points and arguments will be repeated and clarified here—for example, the idea that there is an important difference between global news and global journalism as well as the suggestion that global journalism is not the opposite of local journalism or national news but instead an essential extension of them.

SOME CONCEPTUAL CLARIFICATIONS

- In this book, I will primarily pay attention to global journalism as news and news journalism, i.e., not global journalism as other journalistic genres (for example, documentaries) or media genres (for example, film).
- In most cases, news journalism and journalism will be treated as synonyms.
- The recipients of news journalism are defined as audiences *and* users in order to emphasize their active role.
- Domestic journalism, news and/or news media refer to local and national journalism/news/news media simultaneously. However, in some contexts, such as in chapter 3, I focus on the historical development of national news.
- The global outlook is analyzed in relation to the domestic outlook in which social reality is journalistically interpreted mainly from a local or national point of view. As local communities and territories exist in a national context, the local outlook also tends to include a national one. Thus, when referring to the domestic outlook, I conceptually merge the local and national outlooks (in which domestic refers to both simultaneously). However, in some cases, as in a particular section of chapter 3, I analyze the national outlook in particular. The global outlook is also understood in relation to the foreign outlook, i.e., the tradition of covering the world outside the domestic territory in terms of "foreign events" (the global outlook instead seeks to illuminate how the foreign event is intertwined with domestic conditions and/or processes in other parts of the world).

2.

So What Exactly Is Global Journalism?

Globalization is characterized by transnational and cross-continental relations generated by trade, technology, pollution, politics, armed conflicts, media, energy supply, etc., while global journalism is supposed to cover these relations. But more precisely what does this kind of news look like? There is only one way to challenge the idea of global journalism as a myth (Hafez 2007)—to de-mystify it by placing the empirical cards on the table and to exemplify its presence in the news. First, we should not think of global journalism as something entirely different—only slightly different—from the kind of news that dominates the everyday news flow. Second, global journalism studies usually involve a selection of cases from numerous countries around the world as in the volumes edited by de Beer & Merrill (2008) and Löffelholz & Weaver (2008) or in several other books on global journalism. However, in this context, global journalism is not studied in terms of comparisons between media systems (Hallin & Mancini 2004) or journalism cultures but is rather explored as a concrete and potentially "universal" journalistic practice. In order to emphasize that global journalism studies are not necessarily synonymous with engagement in "international comparisons" but rather with the analysis of a particular kind of discourse in the news, I will concentrate on the coverage of global crises and issues emanating (only) from one particular country's news media (the Swedish news press, in most cases Web editions). On the one hand, Swedish news media perhaps make a typical case, as they, like news media in most other countries, tend to primarily marginalize "global society" and highlight traditional local and national outlooks. On the other hand, Sweden, as a country, is endowed with a strong platform for global journalism and its development; its newspaper business is in crisis but not to the same extent as in the US and several other countries; there is a strong public service culture (The Swedish Public Service Radio Broadcasting and Television Companies, SR and SVT); international/foreign news is still an obligatory element in mainstream news production, and the Internet connectivity is very high: approximately 85% of the population over 16 years old have access to it (Findahl 2010). And last but not least, Sweden is very dependent on the surrounding world, not least in terms of export and trade (thus, in many respects, it needs global journalism).

More precisely, this chapter begins with the presentation of three examples of global journalism, which are explained by means of the concepts of relationships/involvement, inescapability, and concreteness. This is followed by a concentration on the cognitive categories of space, identity, and power (cf. Berglez 2008), and their relevance for the empirical identification of the global journalistic practice in the coverage of various crises and issues. As an important complement to the focus on the epistemological foundation of global journalism, i.e., the global outlook, ontological aspects are handled, and, more precisely, the relation between global journalism and globalization. In relation to the recent "mediatization debate" in media and communication studies, it is important to distinguish between intra- and extra-global elements in news journalism. The chapter concludes with a detailed examination of how global outlooks interplay (or could interplay) with domestic and foreign outlooks in news reporting.

RELATIONSHIPS AND INVOLVEMENT

THE LEAST GUILTY—THE MOST PUNISHED (Arusha) (*Dagens Nyheter*, quality newspaper, www.dn.se, Nov 29, 2009)

Western emissions are the major cause of climate change, but Africa has suffered the most from them. Before the Copenhagen conference, the continent is demanding financial compensation for the damage, money that one hopes will save Tanzania's rainforest.

Without doubt, Africa contributes very little to the greenhouse gas emissions that cause climate change. At the same time, Africa is the continent that is perhaps most vulnerable to its consequences and least equipped to handle them. In Tanzania and 30 other African countries, the emissions are less than half a ton per capita, while EU's approximate emissions are just above 8 tons and the US emits approximately 24 tons of greenhouse gases per capita a year. This is one of the most important points for the African delegation at the climate conference in Copenhagen, where it is hoped that the industrialized countries will undertake commitment to sharply reduce the emissions in the future as well as to compensate Africa for the damage already done. "We are not the guilty ones, but we are affected by what happens. You need to consider what is fair at the international level," says Richard Muyungi, Tanzania's climate negotiator.

So What Exactly Is Global Journalism?

"The prolonged drought in Tanzania has hit stock farmer Daniel Lonyary hard. In one year, 300 of his 500 cows have died." Per-Anders Pettersson/Dagens Nyheter/Scanpix/Sipa Press.

At first glance, the above news item on the global crisis of climate change looks like traditional foreign correspondence: two Swedish journalists in Central East Africa are reporting a Tanzanian ecological catastrophe to Swedish readers. The fact that this news coverage might become confused with foreign journalism is not very surprising. I have defined global journalism as foreign journalism's younger cousin (Berglez 2008) as they are both concerned with the world "outside" the national territory. But this is not foreign news. It would have been the outcome of foreign journalism provided that it would have been reported as a Tanzanian event without any concrete connections to the surrounding world. But as a global crisis, climate change is the overall framework of the event and the main cause of the environmental situation in Tanzania, and the "foreign" rationale is transcended. Thus, the coverage is centered on the *relationship* between the environmental situation in Tanzania, its neighboring countries (the droughts) and "the Western world," and this is what transforms it into global journalism. According to the material in the news story above, the climate problem in Africa is caused by the Global North, i.e., the developing countries ("the continent is demanding financial compensation for the damage, money that one hopes will save Tanzania's rainforest"), introducing a power relationship between The Western powers and the Global South (developing Africa), implying that "Social inequalities and climate change are two sides of the same coin" (Beck 2010: 257). However, if a local journalist from Arusha, Tanzania, wrote more or less the same story and from more or less the same angle, it would probably primarily be taken as a local news story. But, an important point here is that, also, in such a case, it could be viewed as global journalism. As global journalism involves relationships between events and problems across the world, it tends to be produced by different kinds of journalists, local as well as foreign reporters. To some extent, the above (relational) news story helps us view the mainstream kind of news reporting from the outside. More precisely, it becomes evident that most news is *not* globally oriented but instead based on an atomistic rationale in which the world appears as a system of loosely connected continents, regions and nations and probably even more often as a complex collage of rather disconnected events and processes (Berglez 2004, 2006). In some sense, global journalism is nothing but a forceful questioning of this kind of "derelational" thinking in Western news production (see also chapter 3).

In order to understand the relational nature of global journalism, it is necessary to clarify the difference between identification and involvement. A basic assumption in much news journalism is that intercontinental relations are difficult and time-consuming: that it is hard work to connect places and peoples across the world, to demonstrate the interdependency of people living in Stockholm and those in the rural regions of Tanzania. The assumed challenge for the news journalist is to quickly "invent" a relationship which might possibly attract the news audiences/users and attract their attention. A common approach is to offer them something to identify with, for example, a domestic angle or personality or to emphasize universal emotions which anybody could feel or imagine such as human loss, pain, or suffering (see Höijer 2004). However, the more elements of identification in the news story, the more it is implied and indirectly admitted that there is *no* obvious relationship between the reported event/problem and the news audiences/users (as the relationship needs to be "invented"). In other words, often when covering distant human catastrophes or social issues, journalists seek to bridge the assumed gap and non-connection between "us" and "them" by using identification as their main tool. Often, the "moralizing effects" of the news story (Chouliaraki 2004: 185) guide the process of identification and establish the (moral) duty to do something about the situation (Boltanski 1999; Chouliaraki 2006). Importantly, in these contexts, it is very much up to the news audiences/users to decide whether or not they want to see themselves as part of the covered issue or problem. In contrast, global journalism establishes a stronger type of identification process. Instead of merely proposing an ethical relationship between, for example, peoples in Sweden and Tanzania, it instead tends to point out an interdependent relationship between the reported subject/object and the news audiences/users. The Swedish "receiver" of the news story is inscribed in the story from the very beginning: "Western emissions are the main cause of climate change, but Africa suffers the most from them." Global journalism illuminates the way in which the news audiences/users are part of, or involved in, particular cross-continental problems. This does not mean that ethical identification is excluded in global journalism (see Ward 2005, 2008), but ethics is not the salient aspect. You are not asked to engage yourself ethically in the Other (nation, region, person, etc.) and reach out to the Other because you are part of the Other: you *already* have a social relation with the stock farmer Daniel Lonyary in Tanzania (the man in the photo) although you have never seen him before and despite the fact that you will probably never meet. As a Swedish news consumer, you are somehow there, in Tanzania, not in the traditional physical sense, but as a potential polluter, consumer, producer, etc. For the news audiences/users, ethical deliberation comes into the picture in the following way: should I accept my involvement in the current relationship and do something about it, negotiate with the journalistic claim and argue against it ("This is not true as climate change is a hoax!") or simply repress it ("I do not really care")?

The difference between the global outlook and the cosmopolitan outlook

The above presentation is helpful in understanding the difference between a global outlook and a cosmopolitan one. The latter concept has been often applied in the analysis of the news coverage of distant suffering (Chouliaraki 2004, 2006; Höijer 2004) in humanitarian crises and catastrophes (Robertson 2010; Pantti et al. 2012; Cottle 2012). Generally, the cosmopolitan outlook concerns media's ability to promote identification with the different and/or "distant other" (who might be portrayed as a victim), in which difference and distance (Derrida 1978) might involve an ethical, geographical, cultural, religious, or ethnical barrier which needs to be crossed before a bond can be established between "us" and "them,"—between myself and the Other—and the construction of a common "we" (universalism). The global outlook, on the other hand, primarily pays attention to the interdependent relations between "us" and "them" which exist irrespective of, or prior to, such identification (science's conclusion that Planet Earth and humankind are under threat; the relation between a producer and consumer in a global capitalist system of commodity exchange, and so forth).

Table 2.1. The Difference Between a Global and Cosmopolitan Outlook

Global outlook	Cosmopolitan outlook
Social, material, economic, environmental, cultural, technological, etc. interdependence between peoples across nations and continents as basis for the understanding and explaining of human relations.	Identification with the Other as basis for the understanding and explaining of human relations across distant and different nations.

However, in Beck's sociology (2006), the standard philosophical definition of a cosmopolitan outlook is combined with a more social scientific one, which suggests that the identification of interdependent relations between peoples across nations and continents should be seen as part of an cosmopolitan outlook as well (see Beck 2006: 18). Thus, the latter (social scientific) part of Beck's definition tends to remind us of this book's definition of a global outlook.

INESCAPABILITY

Global journalism often appears in the form of global crisis reporting (Cottle 2009a) and below you will find an example focusing on the nuclear threat.[1] The news story as it appeared in the largest Swedish tabloid, *Aftonbladet* (www.aftonbladet.se), involves the ongoing production of nuclear weapons and the possible victims: "NUCLEAR WEAPONS COULD DESTROY THE WORLD —IN 15 MINUTES" (March 30, 2010). The topic is introduced as the "forgotten threat" from the 1980s, while an important background to the story is the upcoming (in the spring of 2010) conference on nuclear weapon security in Washington, DC. Perhaps as a sign of the post-9/11 culture, a terrorism angle is added: "What happens if terrorists get access to homemade atomic weapons that could kill hundreds of thousands of people?" In order to emphasize the presence of a potential global crisis, a map is included which shows where nuclear weapons exist and to what extent:

So What Exactly Is Global Journalism?

"Nuclear weapons could destroy the world – in 15 minutes." March 30, 2010.
Image/ graphics: Aftonbladet (Web edition).

> During the Cold War, a possible nuclear war was the great threat against our world. In contemporary times, we are afraid of climate change. The climate change can kill our planet in the long term, but nuclear weapons can kill us in a few minutes.
>
> Today, it is very silent about this threat. Very silent. The climate threat is seen as the most acute threat that endangers the existence of our planet. The greenhouse gases are a real threat in the long term, but nuclear weapons are a total nightmare that could strike within a few hours.
>
> A heavy light that burns our eyes from a long distance. This is the first thing that happens in a nuclear explosion. Next is the enormous blast that kills everything within its radius. It blows up eardrums and lungs on those who stand out of range. It smashes buildings. The heat from the explosion is so high that bodies could vaporize. Those who survive risk serious burn damages. Add to this, the radioactive radiation that kills immediately or over many years. Luckily, one does not think about all this too often…how close the world is to its own holocaust. Probably, it is because we do not see all these people who, day after day, go to underground command headquarters and closely guarded laboratories in order to play with life and death.

The above news extract witnesses the ways in which potential global crises might strongly interact with media logic (Altheide & Snow 1979; Berglez 2011a) and a commercial rationale: Despite the fact that *Aftonbladet's* Wolfgang Hansson is, in my view, a very skilled and experienced foreign correspondent, to portray the world in such pessimistic fashion is a very "tabloid" thing to do ("...how close the world is to its own holocaust"; "...nuclear weapons can kill us in a few minutes") and tries to trigger public fear by emphasizing that our fate is in the hands of mysterious "...people who, day after day, go to underground ...headquarters and closely guarded laboratories in order to play with life and death" (cf. Furedi 2002; Altheide 2002). However, this coverage could be seen as an extreme, or perhaps pathological, example of what global journalism often tends to generate, which is a *discourse of inescapability*, in which the news audiences/users are supposed to realize that seemingly distant global mechanisms—nuclear threat, climate change, economic crimes on the Internet or pandemics—could threaten, annoy, control, or reach them wherever they might be situated on Planet earth. Even if we live our everyday lives in our domestic, ethnic, middle-class, etc. cocoons, at least for a moment, global journalism manages to tear down the territorial borders which nations and peoples set up, orient, and protect themselves with. It might also reveal that powerful countries' and territories' efforts to exclude unwanted elements are not only morally illegitimate but vain and desperate as well from the US-led anti-terrorism security efforts to the EU's "Schengen Wall." Global journalism tends to imply that we are all in the same boat heading for destruction, not just on particular occasions (such as the Cuban Missile Crisis in 1962) but more or less *all the time*. A global threat such as the nuclear holocaust is shrinking the world into one small place and fills Marshall McLuhan's concept of "global village" with unpleasant substance (McLuhan and Powers 1992). In my view, McLuhan's concept primarily seems to generate a positive vision of a future world in which the global dimensions of life are inescapable (again, in a positive sense), in which people communicate and bond with each other across territories, creating a new and exciting world, including the kind of fraternal global village culture that social media are supposed to finally establish—at least in theory (for example, Twitter's homepage states that "Twitter Inc believes the open exchange of information can have a positive global impact"). However, due to the nature of news production and its inherent news values (see chapter 4), the

So What Exactly Is Global Journalism?

inevitable global world will always primarily involve the dark sides of globalization, possibly triggering anxiety and fear (Cottle 2009a). As Beck (1992) and Giddens (1990) have pointed out, the more knowledge and information about the global world that is produced, including its possible risks and threats, the more anxiety will result, especially among youth and children (Ojala 2007).

Inescapability is the element that takes global involvement to the next level. It is global journalism's demonstration of Planet Earth as potentially a claustrophobic and catastrophic place, which, again, sheds light on the way in which "ordinary" (non-global) news journalism tends to work. Global journalism's generation of information, imagination, and/or feelings of inescapability is simply not possible in the context of traditional local journalism or foreign correspondence. The framing of these kinds of news is based on the assumption of an *outside*, that is, some *other* place, be it another country, region or continent. More precisely, in news journalism in general, social reality is reported as demarcated domestic, regional, or continental areas (Roosvall 2005), which means that there is always some safe haven, a place to escape to. However, we all know that, in reality, a majority of the world's people have limited chances to escape their problems, be they wars, humanitarian catastrophes, slavery contracts, or human trafficking.

Consequently, when it comes to, for example, the global crisis of climate change or risks of post-Soviet nuclear weapons going astray, global journalism tends to communicate that no matter which part of the world we are talking about, Stockholm, Calcutta, or the pampas of Argentina, the place is potentially dangerous, and *all* people are more or less involved and threatened. As Beck puts it: "The greater the planetary threat, the less the possibility that even the wealthiest and most powerful will avoid it" (Beck 2010: 258). It is possible to imagine how the wealthy, the elites, might spend their money to flee to another planet in a spacecraft or decide to circulate in outer space until the threat is gone. Perhaps, global journalism's inbuilt tendency to point towards a state of inescapability is counterproductive, creating nothing but fear and paralysis; but perhaps this mode is necessary in order to establish a global political culture (glopo culture) of increasing political engagement and interest in global sustainability issues (see chapter 3). To put this matter in somewhat futuristic terms: ideally global journalism, along with many other types of efforts and actions, might help to avoid, or at least delay, our mass exodus to Mars.

CONCRETENESS

For better or worse, to identify global *crises* and to indicate that they present a great danger to the entire planet seems to be the natural way of translating "global reality" to media logic (Berglez 2011a). However, some global relations, for various reasons, cannot be "packaged" as crises, such as social or political affairs of the less spectacular kind which witness globalization's integration in people's everyday lives. The presence of these *global issues* in the news is based on the journalists' ability to reconnect seemingly disconnected events on separate continents and in different contexts in one and the same news story, such as the Swedish news story below on the production of computer game controllers in China and the consumption of these products in Western countries:

> **MICROSOFTS'S WAGE: 3 SEK AN HOUR** [3 SEK is approximately 0.35 EUR] (*Aftonbladet*, www.aftonbladet.se, April 18, 2010)
>
> **Photos smuggled out of the factory in southeast China: "Sounds like torture."**
>
> To not be able to keep your eyes open during the 10-minute break. 15 hours in 30 degrees Celsius forces the workers in Xbox factory to take every chance to get some sleep.—"When I first heard about it, it sounded like torture," says a human rights representative.
>
> Toilet visits are not allowed except during breaks at the KYE Systems Factory in Dongguan in south China. Here they produce game controllers for Xbox. 30% of the products, such as computer mice and webcams, are produced for Microsoft, *The Daily Mail* reports. For less than 3.50 kronor per hour, men and women work up to 15 hours a day, 6 or 7 days a week. Sometimes with 1000 persons squeezed into a space measuring 32 x 32 meters.
>
> The photo is from the human rights-oriented NGO, NLC, which is dedicated to stopping sweatshop factories and bad working conditions. "It sounded like torture. The extreme speed at the assembly line and the same monotonous movements again and again for twelve hours or more," says Charles Kernaghan at NCL, who has published a report about the conditions at the factory.

So What Exactly Is Global Journalism?

"Sleeping at their lunch break. The workers try to get some sleep during their 10-minute lunch break. Their days can be 15 hours long and toilet visits are not allowed." April 18, 2010. Photo: The National Labor Committee

Microsoft is a major global company with millions of customers, and the news story emphasizes the exploitation of its workers, in which the news audiences/users might participate as potential users of game controllers and computer mice. Thanks to this news coverage, the "Made in China" label, which is visible on so many consumer products, expresses human exploitation and suffering. An obvious link is established between the computer mouse on my office table and the working conditions in a Chinese factory.

The above news extracts demonstrate global journalism's ability to make globalization rather concrete. It is a fact that, in local, as well as in foreign news reporting, globalization and its processes, crises, and issues in most cases tend to appear as a quite abstract. "The global" is presented as background information, as an overall context, as statistics or as a "distant phenomenon" which is only partly relevant to an understanding of the reported event. Therefore, in the news, domestic and foreign realities often seem concrete while global processes such as the global market economy or climate change become somewhat less so. It is as if the domestic and foreign realities are obvious, in contrast to the less obvious global reality, which the journalist (who always suffers from a lack of time and resources) finds hard to detect. But the global is not some complex distant reality as it is present *within* the local, national, and foreign. The idea that the "global is local" may sound like a cliché, but it is at least a very true cliché. When a global issue is embedded in the news as in the above example, globalization becomes as concrete as any other aspect of reality and is seen as directly connected to our everyday lives, habits, and (consumer) behaviors. Global journalism is thus a mode of news reporting that reveals the falsity of the assumption that the relationship between the global and local corresponds to the relationship between the abstract and concrete. In other words, its journalistic language challenges the idea of global-local as abstract-concrete. What thus distinguishes global journalism from much of mainstream journalism is its general ability to deal with global processes in accordance with similar journalistic conventions and routines that are applied by ordinary domestic and foreign journalism. So, if the above news story on the Chinese factory seems like ordinary news, it could be seen as a sign that a global condition (market capitalism) has become integrated into the familiar and established media logic (instead of appearing as an abstract, distant force). In other words, what is basically a discursive niche (the global outlook) appears as a "non-niche" due to the concrete and obvious disguise of globalization in the news. An indication of whether or not a news story has succeeded in making a global process concrete and relating it to peoples' everyday lives ought to be the amount of reader commentaries and reactions. The news story on the Chinese factory generated hundreds of comments, i.e., UGC (user-generated content), on *Aftonbladet's* news web:

> This is the true face of capitalism. The problem is that these things are always portrayed as particular cases of bad working conditions, and not as what they are: a necessary part of the capitalist system whose central characteristic is exploitation of humans. (Sybok, 100 years old)

So What Exactly Is Global Journalism?

> Damn, I already boycott Apple, and now this. So what other alternatives are there... any suggestions from computer nerds out there? I don't want to contribute to slavery. (Uncle Tootie, 55 years old)
>
> This is the consequence of Communists' rule. The citizens are treated as cattle, their lives belong to the State. (Tothal, 107 years old)
>
> Why do you think that the Swedish manufacturing industry will soon be outcompeted by the Chinese? It is not because of the quality. Ask yourselves next time you buy cheap commodities: how can the prices be so low? Slavery is cheap, child slavery as well. (Farmartanken, 61 years old)

Such comments from the public also demonstrate that global journalism's establishment of concrete relationships, such as the (potential) one between the Chinese workers and the readers of the *Aftonbladet*, transform global news from being matters/news à la *The Economist* for a few enlightened members of the elite to a more popular kind of political discourse (Dahlgren and Sparks 1993; see also chapter 3) in which the global issue generates broad and diverse engagements, involving consumption behavior and morality ("Damn, I already boycott Apple, and now this..."; "Ask yourselves next time you buy cheap commodities: how can the prices be so low?"); domestic outlooks on and concerns about the global market economy ("Why do you think that the Swedish manufacturing industry will soon be outcompeted by the Chinese?") as well as ideological reasoning ("This is the true face of capitalism"; "This is the consequence of Communists' rule").

THE GLOBAL IS YOU AND IT'S OBVIOUS (THE LEITMOTIV OF GLOBAL JOURNALISM)

It's you

Naturally, much news reporting on global relations does not directly involve or concern the news audiences/users themselves. But still, a major feature of global journalism is its boomerang rationale in which the news story, via some covered subject/object, begins and ends with the news audiences/users themselves. To personalize the news and to somehow engage the news audiences/users at the private level are fundamental features of news journalism in general (cf. Berglez 2006: 105–112). In some sense, global journalism tends to represent an extreme form of this very formula by seeking to engage the news audiences/users, not only personally and privately in the covered matter but as one of the main *actors* in the coverage. The news audiences/users are rather brusquely pulled into the globalizing reality as consumers of a mouse pad, as everyday CO_2 emitters, as potential victims of a nuclear accident or war, and as Internet users, tourists, producers, or exploiters, while this is possibly gradually establishing a social reality based on the idea that, as individuals and as a collective, we are very often part of a bigger context.

It's obvious

Basically, global journalism is a relative of hardcore business news and its inbuilt ability to transcend all kinds of borders in its stock market reporting and instant coverage of the global flow and transactions of capital[2] (see also chapter 3). However, in the financial news discourse of, for example, the Dow Jones newswire (www.dowjones.com) and Bloomberg (www.bloomberg.com) (cf. Machin & Niblock 2010), man and society are repressed, or to speak in Marxist terms, reified, in terms of figures and graphs, as well as squeezed into a global news style which "...avoids culturally specific emotive responses" (Machin & Niblock 2010: 795), while in global journalism, the rather abstract financial rationale is exchanged or complemented with extra-economic content, involving *peoples'* life conditions and social conflicts of various kinds. In other words, here, economic abstraction is replaced by social flesh. Global journalism is working at its best when global reality is taken down from the abstract skies to the concrete empirical ground in such a way that its obvious impact on society and everyday life mercilessly shines through the news discourse.

GLOBAL SPACE, POWER, AND IDENTITY

It is possible to get a deeper understanding of the above aspects of global journalism by focusing on *space, power and identity* (Berglez 2008, 2011b), as these central cognitive categories make the global processes rather visible in the news. To begin with, globalization essentially involves transformation of space (Morley 2000). The global economy, rapid and frequent travel, the speed of technology, etc., tend to make the world smaller and connect previously or seemingly disconnected spaces, materially, socially, ecologically and culturally speaking. Here, we should also include possible resistance to transnational transformations of space, which might involve both xenophobic exclusion of immigrants and/or transcultural influences and the protection of domestic territory from globally initiated material exploitation or environmental pollution. This leads us to power, which in the global context might concern power

So What Exactly Is Global Journalism?

relations as well as frictions between nation-states and global conglomerates or institutions or between the individual and the power structures of global capitalism (Bauman 2000). Finally, globalization involves identity processes, in which the market, travel, ICTs, media, etc., establish interconnections between peoples worldwide and pave the way for global identities as well as frictions between various identity formations, for example, global vs. local, global market-oriented vs. anti-capitalist, or cosmopolitan vs. nationalist identities (Olausson 2009a; Morley & Robins 1995). Thus, it ought to be possible to detect global journalism in the news by posing the following empirical questions (Berglez 2008: 245):

Table 2.2. Space, Power, and Identity in Global Journalism

Journalistic representation of:	Empirical questions:
Space	In what ways and to what extent is there a multi-faceted geography in which journalism interrelates processes and practices simultaneously occurring in separate places worldwide?
Power	In what ways and to what extent are topics and conflicts explained as a complex mixture of domestic, foreign, and global powers?
Identity	In what ways and to what extent does news journalism cross national and continental borders when representing (political) identities?

Space

News events primarily tend to take place *elsewhere* unless you are a media celebrity who constantly generates news—at least this is the case most of the time for most people. This becomes evident in the case of foreign news, as the very point with foreign correspondence is to deliver information from some distant country or part of the world. If we reconnect to the news story from Africa, from a Swedish perspective, Tanzania might seem a very distant place in the southern part of the world. But in global journalistic practice, the distant space is simultaneously "here" too, and what goes on in Swedish home space potentially affects Tanzanian space as well. Due to cultural, mental and historical barriers, the foreign correspondent's obligatory spatial distinction between internal (home) and external (foreign) space is present in global journalism as well, but it is weakened and more blurred when, as here, internal space is built into the reporting of external space, and vice versa. One could say that global journalism seems to be an attempt to take on a spatial perspective that has traditionally been repressed by the news media, which is, to discursively emphasize that in a globalizing society

> ....place becomes increasingly *phantasmagoric*: that is to say, locales are thoroughly penetrated by and shaped in terms of social influences quite distant from them. What structures the locale is not simply that which is present on the scene; the "visible form" of the locale conceals the distanciated relations which determine its nature. (Giddens 1990: 19)

Sometimes global journalism even makes spatial distinctions disappear. For example, the above nuclear weapons article is not linked to any particular space; it is not even domesticized (from a Swedish point of view), which is otherwise a rule of thumb in news media production (Riegert 1998; Clausen 2004). In this respect, but only in this respect, global journalism becomes a global version of local journalism, taking on the mission to construct a neighborhood consisting of seven continents (Berglez 2007: 149–150) in order to implant some proximity at the transnational level.

The global outlook on space in news journalism essentially seems to involve the practice of connecting seemingly disconnected spaces, as in the following extracts from a Swedish local newspaper (*Nerikes Allehanda*) article on food transportation in the world and its environmental results. The idea is to trace and map various groceries' entire journey before they end up in the city of Örebro, Sweden:

> **THE FOOD THAT IS ALWAYS ON THE MOVE** (*Nerikes Allehanda*, November 29, 2009)
>
> Cornflakes from Kellogg's: Corn from Argentina to Bremen in Germany. The finished cornflakes are transported to Stockholm and then to Örebro Country (13,000 km).
>
> Orange juice from Eldorado: Juice concentrate from Brazil to Rotterdam, Holland. Then on to Torsby in Värmland [a region in south Sweden] where the concentrate is mixed with water. From there to Stockholm, and then to Örebro Country (11,000 km).
>
> Salmon/rainbow trout: Cultivated in Norway and then transported via the Mediterranean and the Suez Canal to Bangkok. Filleting and packaging and then transport to Helsingborg (city in south Sweden), followed by truck transport to Örebro Country (17,000 km).

As consumers, we are quite aware that many of the groceries that we buy are produced and prepared in distant places, but the desired effect of this news story is to demonstrate more concretely the cross-continental origin of the salmon or orange juice on our dining tables. Here, the journalist wants not to focus on some events or processes in a particular space but to emphasize relationships between a spatial centre (Örebro) and other spaces (Bremen, Norway, Bangkok, Brazil, etc.). Furthermore, the development of Web news and UGC might help to modify the ingrained idea that news always "happens" in either local, national, or foreign space. During the climate negotiations in Copenhagen (2010), the *Aftonbladet* (on www.aftonbladet.se) arranged a cross-continental chat session on climate change and its effects on the Maldives, which became the main news event (while complemented with some regular articles on the Maldives and climate change). More precisely, Swedish news audiences/users were offered the opportunity to chat with a Maldivian family:

1 PM: CHAT WITH THE SHARIFS—LIVE FROM THE MALDIVES (Dec 17, 2009)

Moderator: Hello, and welcome to the chat session. Aishah Sharif will answer your questions, starting at 1 PM, but you can send your questions now. Feel free to ask questions in Swedish.

Thu, Dec 17, 2009, 11:55

Robert: When I visited the Maldives in the early 90s, I thought it was paradise on Earth. How has it changed since then over the past 20 years?

Thu, Dec 17, 2009, 13:00

The Sharif family: Before, we had beautiful beaches, but these have gradually disappeared, it is not as it once was. The biggest changes happened after the building of the big port. After that, things got worse. Usually, the sand moves with the seasons. When they built the port, the sand could not move in a natural way.

Thu, Dec 17, 2009, 13:04

Maud: Could the CO_2 emissions explain the fact that the Maldives are buried under water, or is it something else? What do you think?

Thu, Dec 17, 2009, 13:06

The Sharif family: We think that climate change is an underlying cause. But also the port, the building project, has to do with it. And climate change is a human product.

Thu, Dec 17, 2009, 13:09

Thus, the Maldives, as a place, become part of global space with a common problem (climate change). The interaction, involving tourism experiences ("When I visited the Maldives in the early 90s, I thought it was paradise on Earth") and the identification of a common global crisis ("...climate change is a human product"), potentially helps to reduce the kinds of mental and cultural barriers which geographical distance tends to generate (imagine and compare with a traditional coverage of a problem in a foreign country).

Power

Power might be defined as the capacity to implement a goal as well as a relation between institutions, groups, and individuals (Peterson 1987: 9; Berglez & Nohrstedt 2009), which involves influence and/or distribution of resources. Global journalism's outlook on power involves micro- and macro-power discourse in various ways. More precisely, one could categorize it in the following way:

1. Relations and/or struggles between global powers: Apple vs. Microsoft, the US vs. the UN, etc.
2. Micro-power acts and their global expansion/development: Here, we need to imagine news stories which, in real time, and/or retroactively narrate how acts or ideas from individuals, groups or organizations at the local level are spreading across continents, establishing reactions, alliances, and power conflicts. A well-known example is the news media's overall coverage of and involvement in the Mohammad cartoon controversy and its chain of events, which originated from Danish Jyllands Posten's publications of certain controversial cartoons followed by numerous micro-power acts around the world (Eide et al. 2008).
3. The relationship between micro- and macro-powers: for example "the little man" or the small local organization vs. the big global institution or company (see Cottle and Lester 2011); the South Korean farmer against the World Trade Organization (WTO); the small country vs. the United Nations Security Council; the Wiki movement vs. the US government, or transnational movements such as Occupy Wall Street vs. global capital.
4. Multi-power news discourse: (1), (2), and (3) might develop and expand into multi-power news discourse in terms of the inclusion of even more

complex political power relations among individuals, groups, organizations, institutions, and companies at the local, national, regional, transnational, and global levels.

Special attention should be paid to multi-power news discourse and its rather advanced journalistic representations of relations. The news story on the KYE Systems Factory in Dongguan could be seen as an example of this, as it includes conflicts between local (the factory, the workers) and global (Microsoft) actors as well as the news audiences/users and their micro-powers as consumers of computer mice and other Microsoft devices. Furthermore, the climate report from Tanzania demonstrates multi-power interplay and conflicts, involving the nation-state of Tanzania, 30 other African countries, the EU, the US, and "Western society" but not least an individual (the Tanzanian farmer and his lack of power at the local level) and the news audiences/users themselves as assumed contributors to the global crisis of climate change. The rationale is as follows: the more journalists and editors are willing and equipped to combine the role of various powers in different parts of the world in one and the same news context and to demonstrate their interrelations, the more globalized the coverage of power. The following small extract from the Swedish quality newspaper *Svenska Dagbladet*, is perhaps an even more obvious case of multi-power news discourse and its relationships:

> **APPEAL TO PRIVACY TO GOOGLE** (*Svenska Dagbladet*, www.svd.se, April 20, 2010)
>
> **Major representatives of ten countries have come together in order to invite Google, the ICT giant, and other Internet companies to resolve the privacy issue.**
>
> On Tuesday, Jennifer Stoddard, Canada's privacy commissioner, said: "While we hear companies as Google talking about integrity in beautiful terms, this is not always reflected in the product marketing." Stoddard reported that an "unprecedented" collaboration between several countries has begun in order to, with one voice, remind the Internet companies to respect the countries' privacy laws. Jennifer Stoddard is one of the signatories of a letter addressed to the director of Google, Eric Schmidt, which expresses its concern that the integrity issues are not respected enough by the company, and especially not in the case of the ICT giant's marketing of Buzz—the ex-

pected competitor to the social network Facebook. The letter to Eric Schmidt is signed by official integrity watchdogs from Canada, Great Britain, France, Germany, Ireland, Israel, Italy, the Netherlands, New Zealand and Spain (NY TT-Reuters).

In this short report on the most rapidly expanding kinds of everyday practices in the developed world, the use of Internet and social media, power at the local (the private Internet user), domestic (of the nation states), and global level (Google) is involved (see Fuchs 2009). Among other things, the possible development of global journalism as mainstream news production is dependent on the expansion of global power discourse in the news. However, contemporary cases such as the regular news reporting of the No. 1 global crisis in the world, climate change, and the investigative reporting on Internet powers such as Microsoft, Google and Apple, which obviously make the world more global by interconnecting peoples across the world more than any other companies and institutions in history, might, in combination, pave the way towards the real breakthrough of the generalization of global outlooks on power in the daily news. On the one hand, it is true that many power issues are not global, but, on the other hand, in most domestic news, irrespective of the topic, it is certainly possible to include at least some element of global power. I am prepared to challenge you: give me any news topic or event, and I will give you the potential global power angle (see also chapter 3).

Identity

Identity involves socio-cultural and socio-cognitive processes (Moscovici 2001: 33-34) in which individuals become integrated and even internalized in common practices and ideas of how to interpret and handle social reality and in the establishment and reproduction of cultures, political groups, organizations, or communities (Olausson 2009a). Simultaneously, identity concerns the individual's self-creation and agency in relation to existing structures (Giddens 1990). Thus, an important aspect of global journalism is its ability to transgress local or national identity formations, i.e., to, as far as the cultural constraints of mainstream news production allow, demonstrate the transnational complexity of identity processes in a globalizing world (Olausson 2005, 2009a; Berglez & Olausson 2011). For newsmakers, domestic

So What Exactly Is Global Journalism?

proximity (i.e., the emphasis on the local or national "we") is essentially important, commercially speaking (see chapter 4). This means that, in most cases, global journalism is only present in the news provided that it does not threaten the focus on domestic identity too much. But global crisis reporting and/or news on global issues tend to open up space for the questioning of ingrained identity horizons (Höijer 2007) as well as for frictions between residual and emerging identities. The article below, involving *Dagens Nyheter's* coverage of a Swedish company's (H&M) treatment of the developing country Bangladesh, is a good example:

> **H&M's TAX IN BANGLADESH: 585 SEK** [approximately 60 EUR] (*Dagens Nyheter*, www.dn.se, June 22, 2010)
>
> Despite the fact that Bangladesh is one of the company's most important plants, the profit machine H&M paid only 585 SEK in corporation tax in 2008 in Bangladesh. Ylva Jonsson Strömberg, secretary-general of the aid organization Action Aid Sweden, is criticizing H&M and the global company's tax evasion. She is demanding that Swedish politicians begin to act.

"In the autumn of 2009, the Executive Director of H&M, Karl-Johan Persson, held a press meeting when the company released its interim report." June 22, 2010. Photo: Pontus Lundahl/Scanpix/SIPA Press.

> H&M is one of the most profitable companies of all time in Sweden. In 2009, H&M's pre-tax profit reached more than 22 billion SEK. This spring, the majority owner, the Persson family, handed out almost 5 billion SEK to themselves. But only a portion of the profit ends up in the countries where H&M's clothes are manufactured. H&M's advanced tax planning in one of the poorest countries in the world resulted in 585 SEK in tax payments. For 585 SEK, one could buy a skirt and a vest in an H&M boutique in Stockholm. Every year, 11,000 women die in childbirth in Bangladesh and poor women are kept in poverty. "I do not think that customers and shareholders want to contribute to this," says Ylva Jonsson Strömberg at Action Aid, who has examined H&M.

The current news discourse stresses an internal conflict: the poverty among the Bangladesh workers vs. thoughtless and regular consumption habits of Swedish consumers. On the one hand, "For 585 SEK, one could buy a skirt and a vest in an H&M boutique in Stockholm," and on the other hand, "Every year, 11,000 women die in childbirth in Bangladesh and poor women are kept in poverty" (see also the previous news item on Microsoft and China). However, one should pay attention to the way in which this potential "cognitive dissonance" illustrates a conflict between national and global identity. The Swedish national identity and the very "Brand of Sweden" are built upon the idea of unique Swedish pop wonders (from ABBA onward), successful export companies such as IKEA and H&M and groundbreaking ICT innovations (for example, Skype and Spotify). Things for Swedes to be proud of. But, this omnipotent Swedish self-identity is here questioned by a Swedish NGO representative (from Action Aid), urging, not a national/Swedish, but a global perspective on H&M, that is, H&M as part of a global capitalist system that is exploiting poor countries—which can then possibly generate identification with Bangladesh and other countries in the same situation. In a previous context (Berglez 2008: 852), I have suggested that the global outlook on identity is produced in at least three ways in the news:

1. *News journalism on various global identity struggles:* For example, market capitalism vs. political regulations (such as the Tobin tax issue); the Bureau of Piracy movement vs. the media industry; Al-Qaida vs. the US and its allies; the Global North vs. the Global South; renewable and green en-

So What Exactly Is Global Journalism?

ergy vs. the oil economy; cosmopolitan politics vs. nationalism and ethnic tribalism, or the open source community vs. Microsoft.

2. *News journalism contributing to a (common) global public "voice" or "people":* The inclusion of verbal comments such as "Biological diversity is entire humankind's responsibility," or "The nuclear weapon issue concerns all citizens in the world," and so forth.

3. *News journalism, discursively connecting or uniting people with potentially similar identities across continental borders, based on political ideology, gender, class, subculture, etc.* For example, news reporting which, by increasing the use of transnational sources (cf. Reese 2008), highlights global identities at the expense of domestic ones by including the *world's* women, environmentalists, gay activists, Social Democrats, Conservatives, etc. (i.e., not just the women in Sweden but all women in the world or alliances of women across continents).

GLOBAL JOURNALISM AS VARIOUS CRISES AND ISSUES

How should one understand the relationship between global crises and global issues in the news? To begin with, global journalism's coverage of a global crisis might gradually become global issue reporting. For example, a crisis might be considered to be over, but some particular issue connected to that crisis might still be considered newsworthy, such as coverage *in the wake of* the swine flu epidemic (H1N1). On the other hand, the routine and established reporting of some global issue might gradually or suddenly develop into global crisis reporting if media owners, editors, and journalists decide to redefine and "repackage" the global issue into a crisis scenario/situation in order to attract more consumers and/or in order to engage citizens and/or warn them about actual dangers. This became the case in several countries in the mid-2000s when news media, due to different factors (the Stern report in the UK; former vice-president Al Gore's worldwide climate campaign, etc.) transformed the reporting of climate science into global crisis reporting, and climate change was increasingly defined as an urgent global crisis (Cottle 2009a; Olausson 2009b). In Table 2.3, I want to clarify the discursive outcomes of global journalism in terms of crises and issues:

Table 2.3. Global Crises and Issues in the News

Media framework	Coverage	Types of cases	For example, the news coverage of:
Global crisis	• of short-term but primarily long-term crises that witness: • a global problem of the urgent kind • some drastic "ongoing global change" (Gundel 2005: 112) • observations of a chain of crisis events and reactions across the world	• climate change • financial meltdowns • nuclear and energy alerts in the world • escalating or uncontrolled pandemics and epidemics: HIV, malnutrition, etc • cultural/religious/political conflicts • wars and conflicts	• the Mohammad cartoon controversy (2005/2006) • the North Pole melting • the swine flu epidemic (2009) • the global spread of extreme weather (droughts, fires, floods) • the financial meltdown (2009) and the following transnational protests (Occupy Wall Street) (2011) • BP and the Gulf of Mexico oil spill (2010) • the Icelandic volcanic ash crisis (2010)
Global issue	• "global reality" beyond global crises • news on the everyday aspects of globalization or global processes; identified events, involving social, political, cultural, ecological, environmental and technological relationships across continents	• consumption, food and transports • cross-continental crime such as trafficking and drug trade • global or semi-global institutions' (EU, AU, etc.) impact on peoples' everyday lives • news on global or semi-global institutions' influence on domestic and regional institutions • the development of the Internet (private integrity, downloading rights and regulations, electronic colonialism, etc.)	• the Pirate Bay lawsuits (2009/2010) • the political game behind the IPCC negotiations in Copenhagen (2009), Cancun (2010) and Durban (2011) • clothing chain H&M accused of exploiting developing countries (2010) • drug trade from Colombia to different parts of the world (2010) • Apple's introduction of the iPad (2009/2010) • The Assange case and the future of WikiLeaks (2010–)

Extra-global and intra-global elements in the news

The reporting on global crises and issues includes extra-global and intra-global elements. Extra-global elements are utterances and actions which help to maintain the distance to the reported global crisis or issue, thereby paving the way for independent reporting. The intra-global elements gear the coverage in the opposite direction in the sense that the reporting is less able to maintain the distance and runs the risk of becoming *involved* in the global crisis or issue. The Mohammad cartoon controversy is a concrete example of this. The publication of satiric cartoons of Prophet Mohammad in a Danish newspaper (*Jyllands-Posten*) in 2005 caused various reactions around the world (cf. Eide et al. 2008). The news reporting (in general) became part of the global flow of information and social media activities, which also influenced the development of the controversy. Here is another example: much of the news reporting on WikiLeaks's whistle-blowing activities and cyberwarfare in 2010, which focused on the political effects, reactions, and consequences of the publishing of top-secret material, tended to be part of the global WikiLeaks campaign as such.[3]

MEDIATION AND MEDIATIZATION OF GLOBALIZATION

The issue of extra-global and intra-global elements intensifies the need to further clarify the ontological relationship between globalization and global journalism. To begin with, globalization represents cross-continental flows and relations of the economic, social, material, technological, ecological, environmental, and cultural kind. Thus, in this context, it is not restricted to phenomena which involve or potentially affect "the entire world" such as the potential global nuclear crisis but extends to all kinds of cross-continental relations that might witness a globalizing society, including the intertwined social material relationship between Chinese factory workers from Chinese Dongguan and European consumers. Global journalism is supposed to cover the various "realities" of globalization, but is always, more or less, also a co-producer of globalization. Globalization has the power to exist without global journalism, simply because its vast "social material whole" exceeds global journalism (you cannot reduce globalization into a "discursive construct" made by journalism and other forms of language use) (cf. Fairclough 2006). But, global journalism cannot exist without globalization. Global journalism needs global phenomena, such as climate change, in order to become relevant. It presupposes a globalizing reality feeding it with various cross-continental flows and relations which are translated into crises and issues in the news.

The relationship between globalization and global journalism could be further understood in terms of mediation and mediatization (Hjarvard 2008; Couldry 2008). An important aspect of Cottle's global crisis reporting research is how "...global crises become variously *constituted within* the news media as much as *communicated* by them" (Cottle 2009a: 2). For example, nuclear weapons exist and have potentially negative global consequences, and therefore, the news media deliver information about this (mediation). However, the production of news on the state of nuclear weapons in the world also leads to mediatization in which its ontological epithet as a global crisis becomes "...actively conducted and constituted in and through media" (Cottle 2009a: 175).

However, global crises and issues might be mediatized in varying degrees. In retrospect, the framing of the swine flu epidemic in 2009 as a global crisis obviously seemed to be a product of heavy mediatization. Despite the numerous deaths, especially in countries such as Mexico, it caused far fewer fatalities than WHO and numerous experts in the news media expected in its initial stages. To great extent, mediatizations could be explained by media logic's (Altheide & Snow 1979) emphasis on the spectacular (reporting global phenomena as extreme, dangerous conditions and/or acute crises/threats: Nohrstedt 2010), but they could also be explained by underlying political agendas, interests and/or traditions.[4]

Global vs. domestic reality

One should not consider the distinction between mediation and mediatization as a distinction between truth and falsity. In my view, mediatizations do involve social constructions of reality (Berger & Luckmann 1966), but it is important to remember that these are present in *all* kinds of news reporting. Mediations always include elements of mediatization. In the news reporting on, for example, the drastic fall of grain prices and its expected global effects, there is an element of mediation (communication which might be relevant if you are in the grain business or affected by it) as well as of mediatization (the inevitable "construction" and discursive promotion of the global market and thus the global side of social reality). The point is that, in this example as well as in media communication in general, it is difficult to imagine mediated information without some kind of mediatizing element.

Due to the seemingly abstract and distant character of global crises and issues it might seem as if the outcomes of global journalism would be more mediatized than, for example, the outcomes of local journalism. However, it would be wrong to see domestic news as "pre-mediatized" and thus more proximate, immediate, and authentic kinds of news (Berglez 2006: 121–134;

So What Exactly Is Global Journalism? 47

2007). In other words, local and national "realities" are hardly less mediatized than global ones. A news report on a car accident which is narrated as a local event automatically "mediatizes" a local reality in which the media help to construct and reproduce the idea that there is such as thing as a local community in terms of a demarcated, common culture. Furthermore, in the same way, the nation-state (the national reality) is very much a product of mediatizations of a (national) common culture and historic heritage (see Anderson 1991; Billig 1995; Wodak et al. 1999; Berglez & Olausson 2011).

GLOBAL JOURNALISM IS POTENTIALLY EVERYWHERE

Finally, we need to clarify where and how global journalism operates and can be empirically observed in relation to more established modes of news and reporting. As has been pointed out previously in this book, global journalism is not restricted to global media such as Reuters and BBC World. Instead, it can appear in many news contexts, including domestic media. On the one hand, the concept of global journalism is needed in order to crystallize the characteristics of globalized news discourse in relation to other types of news and modes of reporting. But on the other hand, global journalism should primarily be viewed as an integrated mode of reporting (Berglez 2007, 2008, 2011b). More precisely, it is possible to consider global journalism as built on various combinations of domestic, foreign, and global outlooks. Naturally, the global outlook is obligatory, but from foreign correspondence it has adopted its interest in international events, while from domestic reporting it has imported the relevance of cultural and geographical proximity in the news.

Table 2.4 demonstrates the way in which global journalism is possibly integrated with both domestic and foreign news (cf. Berglez 2008: 245). In order to make the table as lucid as possible, domestic news includes both local and national news, while foreign news includes both international information (correspondence from another country) and transnational information (news from particular regions). In the table, *news* and *outlooks* are distinguished. Domestic, foreign, or global news implies that the coverage is explicitly presented as either domestic, foreign, or global news—a global news section in a news magazine or when the presenter on the television news explicitly announces: "...and now some global news." Outlooks, on the other hand, are discursive elements of the domestic (local and/or national), foreign, or global kind within various news reports. For example, local news might include a global outlook in the reporting of a local event. In the table, Sweden represents the domestic, which means that the examples are primarily anchored in Swedish news culture, while Google, as a powerful provider of digital information and communication in the world, represents the global actor/issue. Global journalism, supposedly founded on relationships between news and outlooks, could thus be illustrated by means of the following fabricated (albeit realistic) topics:

Table 2.4. Various Combinations of Global Journalism in the News

		NEWS		
		Domestic	**Foreign**	**Global**
OUTLOOK	Domestic	Google Sweden in conflict with Swedish organizations	Google's new data center in Finland—why is it not placed in Sweden?	*How Google is influencing classroom communication around the world, and Sweden*
	Foreign	Swedish Google-users in comparison with Belgians and Germans?	Report from China and its management of Google	*Google's view on privacy—criticized in Canada*
	Global	*The Swedish critique of Google will be spread around the world*	*Internet censorship in China—how will Google defend its involvement in China globally?*	*Is Google determining the future of human communication?*

Domestic news-domestic outlook: This is domestic news, focusing on a conflict in Sweden between domestic actors (Swedish organizations and Google Sweden). Google is a global actor but is here primarily presented in the domestic form (Google Sweden).

Domestic news-foreign outlook: This is domestic news, concentrating on a domestic event (about Swedish Google users), which also includes a foreign outlook (the Swedes compared with the Belgians and Germans).

Domestic news-global outlook: This is domestic news, focusing on a domestic event (the Swedish critique), while it is complemented with a global outlook ("to be spread around the world")

Foreign news-domestic outlook: This is foreign news on a foreign event (data center in Finland), while the foreign report is endowed with a domestic outlook (why not in Sweden?).

Foreign news-foreign outlook: This is foreign news, focusing on a foreign country (China) and an event in this particular country (China's management of Google).

Foreign news-global outlook: This is foreign news on the situation in a foreign country (Internet censorship in China), which is endowed with a global outlook (Google's involvement in China raises questions about its global position and responsibility).

Global news-domestic outlook: This is global news primarily concentrating on the role of Google worldwide, complemented with a domestic outlook (including Swedish classrooms).

Global news-foreign outlook: This is global news on Google's general stance on privacy issues (involving all Google users around the world), endowed with a foreign outlook (reactions from a particular place abroad: Canada).

Global news-global outlook: The "absolute" version of global journalism; global news (on the role of Google concerning human communication) endowed with a global outlook (it concerns human communication around the world).

In the table, the italicized pairs of terms are the news/outlook-combinations, which primarily develop global journalism. In some sense, all combinations include some element of global journalism as they all involve a global actor (Google). However, in the domestic news/domestic outlook and foreign news/foreign outlook combinations, the global aspects of Google are discursively repressed and/or considered less important. Thus, the table could be used to empirically detect and categorize global journalism in the news flow as well as for practically training in possible variants of global journalism. The above illustrations of global journalism are generally and broadly formulated, possibly applicable on newspapers and radio broadcasting as well as television news discourse. However, in my view, the most dynamic combinations and convergence of domestic, foreign, and global news/outlooks could be observed as well as further developed on the news Web and in relation to the digital news culture (cf. Heinrich 2011, 2012). Chapter 5 is devoted to this particular topic.

3.

The Relevance of Global Journalism

In this chapter, I focus on the relevance of global journalism in general, but mainly from a political and democratic point of view. I begin by providing a sociological and historical background to the importance of a global outlook on contemporary society. Then I, by means of relevant social theory emanating mainly from Ulrich Beck, Jürgen Habermas and Nancy Fraser, will distinguish the news journalism of the Westphalian (pre-global) from the post-Westphalian (global) order and present a more extensive argument for global journalism's relevance for the individual (citizenship) and society (its institutions) as well as for the future of news media and news journalism in general. Here, an important aspect is global business news (the "first" kind of global journalism) and how the expansion of global reporting beyond the financial domain could make globally oriented news less elite oriented and help to expand glopo culture in our predominantly national societies. The chapter ends with a discussion on global journalism's innate ability to serve as a constructive (and thus relevant) response to the abyss between news journalism in the Global North and South as well as to the assumed "declining" or at least "liquid" (Deuze 2007), state of professional journalism in the digital era.

BACKGROUND

The Westphalian and post-Westphalian orders

To begin with, it is important to get to the root of the problem that global journalism concretely demonstrates—the conflict between the "old" and "new" society or, more precisely, between the *Westphalian order* and the *post-Westphalian order*. "Westphalian order" refers to the Peace of Westphalia from 1648, in which several European nation-states signed an agreement in which they promised to mutually respect territorial autonomy. Thus, the Westphalian order is connected to the rise and development of the modern nation-state since the 17th century, a process which initially took place in Europe, and then in other parts of the world. It involves the gradual expansion of an international system based on voluntary agreements between autonomous nation-states. Furthermore, the Westphalian order goes hand in hand with a national outlook that nation-states are rather independent and do not allow themselves to be steered by foreign forces and will defend their own ideology. The post-Westphalian order, on the other hand, assumes that nation-state sovereignty has become gradually weakened as a consequence of the development of modern society in the 19th and 20th centuries (Giddens 1990; Beck 2006), and the impact of (global) market capitalism (Harvey 1996). Globalization, which does, however, not only include financial/economic but also social, cultural, political, environmental and media-technological cross-continental processes, has made the nation-state increasingly vulnerable to, and dependent on, external forces which might emanate from complex transnational relations as well as from particular powerful nation-states (such as China or the US). For example, the small nation-state of Sweden is affected by the overall environmental pollution in the world and various transnational economic flows but also by the US as a political and economic agent. The global economy demonstrates that most countries suffer from a post-Westphalian condition, even the big and powerful ones. As Nancy Fraser points out, in the earlier phase of the nation-state (the Westphalian order), "...economies were effectively national and could be steered by national states in the interests of national citizens" (Fraser 2007: 5), but this is no longer the case, as nation-states are intertwined with a global economic system. However, according to Beck (2006), Fraser and others (Held 1995; Habermas 2001), in order to uphold their ability to politically and democratically represent their citizens, nation-states and more precisely their institutions...

1. would somehow need to increasingly admit their far-gone *involvement* in the global world. Instead of referring to the global as an abstract force with only occasional presence/impacts, be it in terms of particular OECD policies or temporal global financial meltdowns, they would need to make "global reality" into an even more natural element in their political discourse. Only this will help nations to steer their future in the long-term, independently and/or commonly through extended international cooperation. Global outlooks need to become fully integrated in the public debate and political decision-making at the national level, otherwise

> the national democratic system will gradually "degenerate" into a residual power-system (as is the case with the contemporary role of the Monarchy whose political actions are merely powerless, symbolic rituals) (Berglez 2006).

2. This could then pave the way for a more *radical breakthrough* for transnational citizenship (Olausson 2005) and political engagement beyond national borders, and in the long term, the development of a cosmopolitan world order; an order, so hard to imagine and define, but still so essential for humankind (Beck 2006).

Most national institutions in the world (governments, parliaments, state organizations, and authorities) will not adopt such post-national changes, simply because it is assumed that the vitality and survival of the nation-state presuppose a continuing *repression* of the global condition. "Global reality" only becomes part of the vocabulary provided that it could serve some (national) political interest. For example, national politicians often justify their inability to act and to change society to the better by referring to global powers (for example, the Swedish unemployment is very much at the mercy of the global economy). Or, when legitimizing certain reforms, they might refer to the importance of keeping pace with the global development (concerning business, education, research, etc.). Thus, one could say that, in many nation-states, there is a *cognitive and discursive conflict* on how to actually conceptualize the world and on how to act in it. Despite the continuing expansion of a post-Westphalian condition, the Westphalian order is thus still rather strong in most countries, which partly could be explained by the simple fact that nation-states and their institutions still exist as separate territories and agents. But according to Beck (2005) as well as Fraser (2007), due to the continually strong reproduction of national outlooks, exaggerated power is attributed to the Westphalian order. The constant equating of society with one's (own) nation-state and/or the sustaining of a strict division between domestic and foreign world/countries despite the deep interconnections between different parts of the world (Beck 2006: 24), tend to support the idea that

> ...humanity is divided into a finite number of nations and that these are organized internally as nation-states, while being demarcated from one another externally in the system of international relations. What is more, this demarcation from the outside world, along with competition between nation-states, represents the fundamental organizing principle of politics. The rationale for belief in the nation-state is, according to thoughtful political scientists in par-

ticular, that democracy has *only* been achieved—indeed, can *only* be achieved—within the nation-state. (Beck 2005: 22)

In (social) sciences, this way of thinking manifests itself as "methodological nationalism," as a particular observer perspective on social reality which unreflectively continues to organize research in terms of national comparisons (Beck 2006: 24). In general, the nation-state view of society is strongly promoted by the symbolic and cultural production of national identity, which helps to repress the entrance of a post-national condition (Berglez & Olausson 2011).

Thus, an important aspect here is that the existence of the nation-state as we know it has to do with belief and stubborn reproduction of this belief. To a great extent, our visions of society are built on social constructions (Berger & Luckmann 1966) and cultural conventions which are embedded in language use (discourse) and established ways of framing the world (Moscovici 2001; Billig 1995). This is why the Westphalian order might continue to operate as prime reality irrespective of the fact that underlying material forces and mechanisms draw society in a contrary direction (i.e., toward the post-Westphalian order). But at the same time, social reality is not merely a product of language but involves complex relationships between discursive and extra-discursive (material) processes (Harvey 1996; Berglez 2006; cf. Guy 2009), which makes it difficult to ignore some global mechanisms entirely. For example, nuclear power and financial meltdowns bear witness to the post-Westphalian condition, and no matter how much one might *believe* in the autonomous and untouched status of the nation-state, it is hard to deny that transnational (radial) processes do not affect one's own country as well as other countries.

Consequently, both Beck (2006) and Fraser (2007) make the point that the strong belief in the continuing power of a Westphalian order will make it increasingly difficult for most nation-states to uphold their traditional democratic functions and obligations. The continuing pretense that the global world is limited to occasional threats which could be solved by internal protection systems, and temporal, quick-fix kinds of international cooperation will appear more and more flimsy and desperate. Concerning the relationship between countries and different parts of the world, some kind of paradigm shift is waiting to be unleashed. According to Beck post-Westphalian reality will sooner or later become impossible to ignore for the majority of the world's population. However, nations and their citizens should not wait but should become increasingly "post-Westphalian" *now* and quickly realize that "cosmopolitan" reality (Beck 2006).

Social reality as a complex combination of Westphalian and post-Westphalian beliefs, processes, and actions

We (average citizens as well as experts and politicians) all require ever more information and knowledge on global processes. Theoretically speaking, one should be able to explain society as a whole, and more or less all we do in our everyday lives, in terms of global networks (Castells 1996) and global causal relations and thereby as a post-Westphalian constellation. In arguing for the emergence and existence of a "global village" it is possible to apply meteorologist Philip Merilee's "Butterfly Effect," the assumption that "the flap of a butterfly's wings in Brazil [might] set off a tornado in Texas," i.e., that even our smallest acts could affect life somewhere else on the planet.

However, an important point here is that society cannot, and should not, be reduced to global relations and mechanisms (Rosenberg 2000). Exaggerated reproduction of national outlooks should not be replaced by similarly exaggerated reproduction of global outlooks. Society and its various social relations, traditions, communications, work, education, etc., might to a great extent be determined by domestic conditions rather than by intercontinental and/or global factors. Of course, "...people talk about global things because there are global things taking place in reality" (Guy 2009: 2), but the power of the global is not all-encompassing and unlimited.[1] Instead, global processes operate differently in different contexts (cf. Guy 2009). A small country such as Sweden might in some respects be rather independent of global influences (for example, in terms of its ability to generate innovations to solve particular domestic problems), while in other contexts it might be extremely dependent on actions and processes occurring in other parts of the world (it is sensitive to global financial developments, etc.). Nation-states are in a constant "on and off" relationship with global reality. A particular nation-state might in one context co-produce a global crisis, event, process, or initiative, while in another context it generates counter-global mechanisms.

One could thus also say that the Westphalian (pre-global) and post-Westphalian (global) orders are parallel and/or rather intertwined universes, which are constantly reproduced by nations and their institutions but also by individuals. Here, we could make things more complicated by moving beyond the discussion on national vs. global powers and include local and regional aspects as well. For example, when cheering on Sweden's national football team at the national stadium, I become part of the reproduction of the nation (the cultural idea of a Swedish "people"), its very nation-state (Billig 1995) and the entire international system (the world as relations between nation-states), while when driving home from the football game, the CO_2 emissions from my Japanese car contribute to both local, national, and regional pollution and to the entire global process of climate change. IKEA tends to represent Sweden abroad or, more precisely, Swedish functionalist design. Thus, when buying IKEA furniture I somehow contribute to the reproduction of Sweden culturally as well as territorially speaking (Sweden as an existing nation that is not, say, Denmark or France). At the same time, I contribute to low-wage jobs at the local level among IKEA subcontractors in developing countries but also to these particular nation-states' (India, Indonesia, etc.) household economies and ultimately to the entire global economic system. Besides, as IKEA's production is rather dependent on wood, my consumption might contribute to some job opportunities in the forestry sector but also to the material exploitation of, for example, the Amazon rainforest, and thus to a South American regional problem, which has negative long-term consequences for the entire planet. Consequently, I generate a complex combination of "Westphalian" and "post-Westphalian" "acts."

Global journalism as the provocateur of an inherent conflict in contemporary news journalism

This self-critical and reflexive reasoning on the relative power of global processes could then be applied to global journalism. Despite the assumed demand for global outlooks delivered as concrete events and journalistic storytelling (cf. Jameson 1991: 410–411), a (counter-global) braking system is somehow necessary.[2] Obviously lots of domestic news requires nothing but domestic sources, historic background and explanations. Similarly, much news needs only a local angle. Besides, it is also seems rather obvious that global journalism cannot replace traditional foreign news entirely. Many events in distant/foreign places are highly relevant and newsworthy without any global causal relations. A revolution in Tunisia, a train accident in Argentina, or a drought in Australia might not have so much to do with "global relations" but will still catch our attention and engage us because of, for example, their riveting content (Baudrillard 1982/1997) or for moral and compassionate reasons (Boltanski 1999; Höijer 2004). But again, perhaps more often than we think, news can be both domestic and global. For example, the Swedish news reporting on the tsunami and nuclear catastrophe in Japan in 2011 was primarily covered as a foreign event, but since these events were affecting different parts of the world (including Sweden) in various ways, a global news discourse soon developed as a natural supplement to the foreign news coverage, focusing more on the catastrophe's effect on the world (on the global economy, the world's view of nuclear power, and so forth). To conclude, then, the relevance of global journalism is highly contextual. And this principle applies not only to global journalism but to all kinds of news journalism (including traditional domestic and foreign journalism).

That being said, this book's central concern still remains: the post-Westphalian order is too repressed in discourse, including that of news journalism. Global journalism's marginalized status in the general news flow is the problem. The national outlook (including the local) dominates the news at the expense of the global, which, in turn, helps to reproduce the national outlook in media culture and society as a whole. The national outlook's power in the media market is thus based on numerous news providers' refusal to realize/admit its *limitation* as a relevant mode of covering reality in numerous contexts. The problem is then that, despite the fact that so many things tend to move toward the global in news journalism, the national outlook is *the* unquestioned No 1 "reality." Today, the nation is much more integrated with global powers and processes than 50, 100 or 150 years ago, but news journalism has not been part of or actually embraced this change in terms of a discursive and cognitive development. Social reality becomes more and more post-Westphalian while news journalism still predominately frames society in accordance with a Westphalian rationale, and "...by insisting on its traditional orientation on the nation, journalists are losing touch with a society that is global..." (Deuze 2007: 141; Berglez 2007). Psychoanalytically speaking, then, the national outlook has somehow become the "repressive normality" of mainstream news journalism.

GLOBAL JOURNALISM'S RELEVANCE FOR NEWS AUDIENCES/USERS

Basically, for the news audiences/users, global journalism is ontologically and epistemologically relevant. It is ontologically relevant as it connects us to an important social material reality which would otherwise be rather absent in the news: globalization (Cottle 2009a). Its ontological relevance is closely related to its epistemological relevance as a producer of "global knowledge."

Global journalism enables us to transform the abstract and often invisible nature of the global into news discourse; i.e., into concrete events, crises, issues, relations, etc.

The ontological and epistemological relevance of global journalism leads us to its *democratic relevance*: its potential to provide us with power to affect and/or change particular conditions in our own society and in the world as a whole. In other words, it promotes global empowerment in everyday life and in formal politics and helps develop global citizenship (to see and treat the entire world as a natural platform for political engagement) (Beck 2006; Held 1995). Furthermore, its democratic relevance could be linked to information and action relevance.

Information relevance: It is reasonable to argue that life under globalization, whether in Stockholm, Uruguay, or North Thailand, generates a natural need for professionally produced cross-continental news about all sorts of things: the environment, politics, social issues, health, food, education, the future, cultures, or technology. It requires information about intertwined and/or causal relationships "here" (my home, life, work, community, politicians, health condition, ideas, everyday practices, etc.) and "there" – the seemingly distant "foreign world" (Rantanen 2009: 80) and its dynamics and mechanisms. In other words, global journalism might help us "...to navigate daily life" (Peters & Broersma 2013: 4) in global times.

Action relevance: as a natural extension of information relevance, global journalism also builds on its ability to produce information which helps us to reflect upon as well as organize our actions in a globalizing society. It can deliver alternative and broader perspectives on the proximate and already familiar, on one's home country, local region, or private world/community, and it might help to transcend one's limited worldviews and gridded movements/orientations in the social landscape and on the Web (see Halavais 2000). What makes global journalism different from other types of news is its ability to, in the form of storytelling, transform "de-globalized" (local, national, foreign) views on any subject to a more global view on that subject by incorporating the "bigger intercontinental picture," thereby presenting more action alternatives on how to handle the local/private or political/public issue, event, tradition, etc. (cf. Giddens 1990: 16–17).

Despite its obvious relevance for the news audiences/users, we need to remember that there is no "objective" need for global journalism. Who could actually decide what a person should consume? There are plenty of intelligent reasons for consuming global journalistic news, but some of us occasionally or regularly prefer only hyperlocal news (Kurpius et al. 2010) simply because we see it as the most relevant kind of information for us (see also chapter 4). Besides, our life can be successful and generate a lot of happiness without any news whatsoever, including global journalism. But, on the other hand, this does not undermine my argument that, for those who consume news for the sake of education, cognitive orientation, or gaining power and influence in certain areas, global journalism will become an ever more important source in the future.

As an extension of its relevance for the individual: global journalism is good for society

Global journalism is essential for society and for all kinds of institutions (including authorities and organizations) which include and represent groups of individuals. Most institutions do collect their own information and establish their own communicative networks (which might also be the case for many individuals who use social media). But in an ever more globally complex world, institutions gain from being confronted with, and somehow permeated by, a globally oriented media environment and news. Global journalism might provide local and national institutions with "reflexive" news (Graf 2009; Giddens 1990), i.e., information which makes them understand themselves better in relation to the entire world. And in order to discern the ways in which they are part of the world, they need perspectives which include cross-national and cross-continental relations, trends, developments, threats, and prospects.

RELEVANT FOR NEWS PRODUCTION?

In media sociology, it is conventional to demonstrate that media and journalism need to "improve" society in various ways, not least from a democratic point of view (McNair 2000). However, sometimes, media sociological reasoning might become rather disconnected from the "reality" of news production and the particular conditions of news journalism (Deuze 2007; Berglez 2012). As media and journalism researchers, we often have dreams and hopes about an ultimate and perfect journalism without concerning ourselves too much about who is supposed to deliver it and by what means (cf. Deuze 2004: 285). Besides, and perhaps needless to say, what media scholars see as relevant for citizens is not necessarily considered relevant by media owners, editors, and practicing journalists.

Why is global journalism so relevant for the news producers themselves? In my view, global journalism is relevant because it brings to the surface the question of how *news journalism is supposed to actually conceive and deal with society in the future*. Here, the anticipated argument is that news journalism "needs" global journalism as part of its future development. Due to the intensification of a globalizing society since the 20th century, a radical historic shift is needed in mainstream news production from the traditional, rather nation-state-centered journalism, to the "nation-state-in-the-global-world-journalism." Global journalism's presence in particular kinds of news discourse such as global crisis reporting (Cottle 2009a) forces us to realize that *news journalism as we have primarily known it,* is at a crossroads: will it continue to sometimes ignore global development by remaining in the "national cocoon" from which the surrounding world is predominately covered as distant and "foreign" (reproducing the Westphalian order), or will it instead gradually make the "nation-state-in-the-global-world-journalism" into mainstream news? Such a radical shift would potentially put an end to the idea of local, national, regional, foreign, and global outlooks as competing news realities and niches or at least reduce the present abyss dividing them. We would then be leave behind the era of news *in* the global village, that is, the production of local, national, regional, foreign and global news as separate news areas and move into the new era of news *for* the global village, i.e., news in which these news categories tend to converge:

Table 3.1. The Basic Difference Between News "in" the Global Village and News "for" the Global Village

NEWS "IN" THE GLOBAL VILLAGE (Westphalian order)	NEWS "FOR" THE GLOBAL VILLAGE Post-Westphalian order)
Local, national, regional, foreign, and global worlds/outlooks as separated from each other in news discourse and in the presentation of news	The combination and convergence of local, national, regional, foreign, and global worlds/outlooks in news discourse and in the presentation of news

More precisely, then, which segments of news journalism are supposed to respond to the call for more global journalism? To begin with, global journalism might be practiced by various journalists and reporters in commercial as well as non-commercial contexts (public service media, independent media, and social media). Furthermore, it might be practiced by international news reporters, working for a transnational media company or the national news, but it might also be practiced by local journalists at local newspapers. From a commercial point of view, to what extent global journalism becomes implemented might depend on such factors as the size of the company (available staff), market conditions, the actual news niche, or simply the framing preferences among media owners, editors, and journalists.

In this context, I am particularly interested in global journalism's potential expansion in mainstream news media and general news production (on politics, culture, technology, health, etc.). Consequently, the focus is on contexts in which global journalism could reach broader audiences/groups of users. However, global journalism's approach might not be suited for all kinds of mainstream news. Despite the fact that global journalism's basic rationale would be possible to incorporate in most news, news media companies which only aim to entertain their audiences/users with soft news and scandals (Thompson 2000), will hardly ever find the global outlook to be a highly relevant mode of reporting and/or framing news.

In order to identify the primary addressees of global journalism in the field of mainstream news production, one could use Ekström & Nohrstedt's (1996) ethnographic study of Swedish news companies as a guiding principle. To begin with, Ekström and Nohrstedt selected and identified news companies which more or less clearly expressed ambitions to provide their audiences/users with relevant and ethically correct news. In the following phase, they explored to what extent these news companies actually fulfilled their own ethical aims and standards. Thus, the discovered lapses and deficiencies in the news production were only compared with the news companies' *own* journalistic goals, and not with academic and research-oriented normative ideals on good journalism. If we translate this to the discussion at hand, we see that of existing and potential providers of mainstream news, only those media which *already* claim to be contributing socially and democratically relevant information in today's globally complex society might become part of the global journalism movement. And only these news media could be criticized for marginalizing global journalism in their news.

GLOBAL JOURNALISM IN THE NATIONAL NEWS: PAST AND FUTURE

One more way of further understanding the necessary expansion of global journalism in the post-Westphalian order is to go backward in time and focus on the rise of national news in the Westphalian order. Here, I will deal with two questions: (1) How did news media in emerging nation-states begin to generate a national outlook on society instead of a more transnational or global direction? And (2) Why is economic news (business news) running like a red thread through the modern history of news when we speak of the global outlook? In this context, I will focus on media with a national scope and coverage and their production of a national outlook (I will not refer to the domestic news/outlook, which also includes the local media/outlook).

Concerning the history of national news production, Jürgen Habermas's (1991) seminal work, *The Structural Transformation of the Public Sphere: An inquiry into a Category of Bourgeois Society*, is still relevant.[3] In his study, Habermas theoretically and empirically explores the rise and development of the (national) public sphere, i.e., the independent space between the market and the State in which deliberative communication between autonomous actors and interests in society is supposed to take place (cf. Sennett 1976). In contemporary society, public spheres are primarily associated with non-private places such as squares, streets, and cafes as well as with virtual meeting points such as mass media (Dahlgren & Sparks 1993) and the Internet (Slevin 2000). The birth and development of the national public sphere are intertwined with the rise of national news media, a process which took place in Europe beginning in the 17th century. It looked rather different and emerged at a different pace in different parts of Europe and different nation-states. Habermas sought to establish a theoretical and empirical synthesis of the developments in Great Britain, France, and Germany.

According to Habermas as well as others (Smith 1984), the actual origin of national news as we today know it could be found in the pre-Westphalian period, from the 14th to the early 17th century, which saw the transition from feudalism to the (early) nation-state and emerging mercantilist capitalism. More precisely, the embryo of modern (national) news appeared in the growing *market sector* and in the production of economic information on, for example, transportation routes, market prices, and commodities (Grafström 2004). "As trade and manufacturing increased, news networks of communication were established within the business community and between the major trading centres" (Thompson 1995: 64; see also Rantanen 2009: 27). The ever more refined routines of producing, distributing, and selling market information became crucially important for the later commercial expansion of political news.

Habermas concentrates on the conflict between the private (market) and public (represented by State power) that followed. More precisely, in the 17th and 18th centuries, the animated market activities in many European cities triggered conflicts between the emergent bourgeoisie, who were engaged in the

The Relevance of Global Journalism

market, and the growing power of the State bureaucracy and national economies. While the bourgeoisie wanted the market to be free from State intervention, the increasingly powerful nation-states, in most cases governed by a monarchy, sought to control the market by means of taxes and trade regulations. This, in turn, paved the way for the establishment of a bourgeois public sphere beyond state control (in cafes, salons, etc.), while gradually, its conversations more and more moved from "business discourse" to political discourse and to the development of a critical press. Thus, "the critical journals and moral weeklies which began to appear in Europe in the late seventeenth and eighteenth centuries provided a new forum for the conduct of public debate" (Thompson 1995: 70). By means of the critical press, the bourgeoisie began to challenge the privileges of the monarchy and the nobility by demanding more power and the universal right to vote. To begin with, these political rights only included the bourgeoisie (men engaged in the market and trade), but in the longer term, the critical press and the following revolutions in Europe generated unforeseen democratic processes. Consequently, the establishment of "bourgeois society" in the 18th and 19th centuries paved the way for liberation among other identity groups as well, such as the working class and women.

The "global" origin of national news journalism

Consequently, the contemporary national outlook in the news could be seen as a product of a dialectic process which began with the communicative struggle between the bourgeoisie and State bureaucracy in late 17th-century Europe. But what kind of outlook dominated the news before this? Interestingly, Rantanen (2007, 2009) has suggested that the early (pre-Westphalian) market-oriented news was endowed with globalizing features (or cosmopolitan ones, as Rantanen prefers to conceptualize it). She emphasizes that the "...early news was not originally 'national' or 'international'" (Rantanen 2009: xii–xiii) as it "...was a product of cosmopolitan cities rather than of nation-states" (p. 19). For example, the commercial centers and cities in early 17th century Europe did not only generate transnational news (on global prices, routes, and commodities) but were also transnational in terms of their ethnically, religiously, and culturally diverse inhabitants, which then also influenced the production as well as reception of the information exchange. This condition, along with the fact that the emerging modern nation-state was still not a completely taken-for-granted form of organizing society, paved the way for a rather "globalizing" news environment or at least an inter-continental one.

Drawing on Rantanen's argument, the "globalizing" market information thus gradually helped to constitute (modern) news journalism, but due to the forceful rise of a Westphalian nation-state system, the global dimension was outcompeted by national news media and their national outlook (see also Thompson 1995: 66-67). Or, to be more precise, while most news areas and topics (including politics) were colonized by the national outlook, economic business news managed to remain rather global in scope and coverage. This might be explained by the fact that, throughout the entire historical process from the pre-Westphalian period 500 years ago until the contemporary post-Westphalian condition, the economic system has continually generated a natural need for transnational information (in my view, the economic system has always been, and still is, the most "obvious" kind of global reality).

(Global) economic journalism as discursive and cognitive role model for global journalism

Casting an eye over the contemporary status of global journalism in the national news, and you will note economic news's relative resistance to the national outlook is still in operation. Global outlooks are continually marginalized except in that one field: business journalism. Here, global discourse is quite strong and even central. This book primarily exemplifies existing global journalism by means of political and environmental news in the form of global crisis reporting, but when it comes to cognition, framing, and discursive content, global reporting is primarily present in the everyday business news. Perhaps, it is primarily the business journalist, not the foreign reporter, who knows how to transform globally complex relations among places, practices and processes into concrete information, a practice which, since the invention of the telegraph in the first half of the 19th century, has become ever more rapid and refined (Carey 1992; Rantanen 2009).

For example, the obligatory global news element in Swedish Public Broadcasting Company's (SVT) *Evening News* is in the five minutes devoted to business news. Here, domestic affairs are combined with the latest results from the stock markets worldwide, i.e., the ups and downs from NASDAQ, Frankfurt, Dow Jones (NY), etc., and their impact on the world economy and different regions. The remaining news, on the other hand (politics, culture, science, health, etc.), is generally more geared towards the narrow national outlook and more sharply divided into either domestic (i.e., local/national) or foreign affairs. Thus, in the case of economic news, the global dimension is already *inte-*

grated in the very presentation and content, but other news areas have not yet made the same journey in terms of global integration. In these areas, the global appears as occasional crises (Cottle 2009a) or issues. Perhaps, environmental journalism, with its focus on global relations of climate change or the nuclear threat, is closest to business news (Berglez 2011a) in outlook and treatment.

It is important not to forget that, in national news media's coverage of economic affairs, international and/or global news agencies have been rather important (Thompson 1995: 156; Boyd-Barrett & Rantanen 1998; Rantanen 2009) providers of information. These services are represented today by, for example, Bloomberg (Machin & Niblock 2010) and Reuters, which tend to become role models for national news media's own business news. But, on the other hand, as in the case with national media, other types of news provided by international and/or global news agencies are not yet endowed with the "economic" kind of globally integrated discourse. In other words, AP's, AFP's and similar agencies' world news on political, social, or cultural events do not primarily deliver global outlooks. Their brief items on accidents, elections, or riots might instead often portray the world as a fragmented collage of disconnected events, places, and identities (Jameson 1991; Berglez 2006: 147–155). This also tends to hold for news networks such as CNNi, BBC World and Al Jazeera (Berglez 2008: 848). Consequently, so far in the history of news, it is mainly economic news which has a global outlook.

Historically speaking, then, global journalism might still be in its embryonic and initial phase, being primarily restricted to economic news.[4] Thus, the "globalizing" rationale of the early pre-Westphalian market and the subsequent development of an ever more advanced kind of global business news *is still waiting to explode into a more general journalistic practice in national news production* which could firmly establish the post-Westphalian attitude in public debate and in society as a whole. This would be global journalism *all the way*, so to speak, and global relations would no longer be mainstream only in economic news but in all areas of news in national media.

What determines the development of news journalism seems to be a complex combination of economic and political factors and, of course, human agency.[5] During the bourgeois revolution, the increasing political power of the nation-state triggered the expansion of private economic market information into a critical press, while what ought to "provoke" global journalism to expand outside the area of business news are the ever-intensified dialectics between the nation-state and the politics of the global world; the power of global actors (from OECD to Google) and global crises (from climate change to the nuclear threat) and the unsustainable condition of the global economic system itself (Parks 2009). Needless to say, today's equivalent of the revolutionary bourgeoisie is a much larger social group: it consists of all of us who, as producers and consumers, are involved in the production of a global world, including its problems and crises (Hardt & Negri 2000).

Table 3.2. News and Journalism in the Westphalian and Post-Westphalian Orders from a Global Journalistic Viewpoint

Overall social condition/ period of time	Economic news (in the context of national media production)	News in general (in the context of national media production)
The Westphalian order: the nation-state as a power with relative economic, political, ecological, etc. autonomy/independence in relation to the surrounding world (Fraser 2007) Historical period (Europe): 17th century and onward	The following kind of "news" developed already in pre-Westphalian times: transnational market information on transportation routes, prices, and commodities, involving relations between cities and commercial centers (Rantanen 2007, 2009; Smith 1984) Primarily from the 17th century and onward: economic information generated by the conflict between the market and emerging nation-state power; news on taxes, market regulations, customs laws, etc. (cf. Habermas 1991; Grafström 2004: 2) From first half of the 19th century and onward: the further establishing of international economic information mainly via global news agencies (Boyd-Barrett & Rantanen 1998)	Primarily from the 17th century and onward: extension and broadening of economic news: the development of "public opinions" and a critical press, occupied with economic issues to begin with, and then followed by other kinds of (political) issues beyond market affairs News journalism as part of the symbolic building of the nation-state (Anderson 1991; Svensson 1988) Intensified presence of the "foreign world" in the news via international news agencies from the first half of the 19th century and onward (Boyd-Barrett & Rantanen 1998) and foreign reporting Despite the professionalization of journalism in the 20th century (Schudson 2013), communication is continually divided into domestic and foreign news, and the gradual development of different types of news (diversification) mainly generates information embedded in national outlooks but also local ones

Overall social condition/ period of time	Economic news (in the context of national media production)	News in general (in the context of national media production)
The post-Westphalian order: representing a more mature stage of modernity, capitalism and globalization in which nation-states become more interdependent and intertwined, economically, politically, culturally, socially, ecologically, communicatively and technologically speaking (Beck 2005, 2006; Fraser 2007) Historical phase: from mid-20th century and onward: (intensification of international trade, global communication technologies, global economic relations/trade, travelling, tourism, etc.; intensification of global crises and issues and their social and material impact on humankind (Beck 2005, 2006; Held & McGrew 2003; Harvey 1989)	The global economy as naturally integrated in the news (see Kjaer & Slaatta 2007; Fahy et al. 2010) News involving interrelations between national, transnational, and global financial and economic processes (on stock market results, interest rates, economic effects, and trends across nation-states)	Continually centered on national affairs. Relative lack of global integration The global world is primarily represented in terms of particular (global) crises (Cottle 2009a, 2011) and/or issues A continuing sharp division between domestic (local/national) and foreign news (cf. Hamilton & Jenner 2004)

GLOPO CULTURE IN DOMESTIC JOURNALISM (NATIONAL AND LOCAL NEWS)

National news journalism's importance for the establishment of national culture and the nation-state is comparable to global journalism's importance for the integration of the global condition within our national societies. However, there are some obvious differences. National news journalism helped to shape the nation-state, but global journalism will hardly help to establish a global state or nation "all the way." Another important difference is that, while national news journalism cannot be considered irrespective of national news media and national public spheres, global journalism can be imagined without any connections to global media and a "global public sphere," i.e., as a gigantic common space for communication across all continents (cf. Thompson 1995; Volkmer 1999; Hafez 2007). Naturally, global journalism might operate in those networks (Al Jazeera, CNNi, and so forth), but, again, I would like to emphasize that its natural home should be *domestic* media (i.e., national journalism but also local journalism).

Hence, what makes the comparison tricky is the potentially converging relationship of the domestic and global. Global journalism might be relevant for the development of news media and journalism in general, but it is primarily essential for the development of the domestic public spheres and news media. A strong argument is that, as the majority of the world's news audiences/users consume domestic news, media have a great responsibility to further introduce the global world in their news. The proposed idea here is that global journalism could contribute to *a new epoch* in the history of domestic news and its political and democratic relevance. I do not see global journalism as replacing domestic news or simply as post-domestic news. I instead see it as an essential ingredient in the future of domestic news.

More precisely, global journalism involves the necessary expansion of *glopo culture from within nations* (Berglez & Olausson 2011) and their news media. *Glopo culture* indicates something stronger and even more basic than a global outlook. Not only does it involve the internalization of the global world in the national context in a more radical way than has been the case to date but also a regular journalistic delivery of "global relations" in all kinds of (domestic) mainstream news in order to stimulate political reactions, ideas, actions, demands, and struggles beyond national borders. The concept of culture then refers to global journalism's cognitive and discursive efforts to transform global thinking into everyday political thinking and acting, i.e., into a cultural phenomenon (cf. Gerbner 1969).

Perhaps one could see the possible establishment of glopo culture in the domestic news as the first small step towards a sustainable global engagement among the world's nation-states beyond their elites. The breakthrough of regular consumption of global news media and the establishment of a "real" global public sphere somehow depend on the hard preparatory work of numerous domestic news media and their integration of a global political culture within the nation-state by means of global journalism. In order to interest the world's nation-states and their populations in taking a serious step out in the world and becoming part of more extensive global cosmopolitan conversations and political institutions beyond today's UN, global journalism needs to converge with the discourse, mindsets, and traditions of domestic news media organizations (and vice versa).

More precisely, global journalism's implementation of glopo culture in the news and domestic news in particular is a project which establishes the world as an integrated reality among the general populace and reduces the gap between the news journalism of the South and that of the North.

1. Glopo culture must play a larger part in news journalism in order to establish the global world as an integrated reality among "the people" (the majority population).

Table 3.3. The Two Main Types of Global Journalism and Their Characteristics

Economic global journalism	**Extra-economic global journalism**
Elite	Mainstream and/or popular
Regular flow of global outlooks	Irregular flow of global outlooks
The global world: integrated condition	The global world: less integrated condition

As has been pointed out, economic news tends to be more globally oriented than other types of news. In the general news flow, then, globalization is primarily synonymous with the global economy and the often abstract market information on cross-continental financial transactions, actions, reactions, and their economic consequences. Global journalism in the form of economic news thus tends to cover a lot of elite institutions (Kjaer & Slaata 2007), such as OECD, IMF, and the World Bank. One could thus define this type of global journalism as *elite* news, primarily intended for and consumed by the "business class." This is why economic global journalism might also be viewed as "journalism from above" (cf. Berglez 2011b: 144–145). Bloomberg, *Business Week*, or the *International Herald Tribune*, and their numerous disciples in national business editions, tend to be endowed with market capitalist values in which the reports on flows and transactions of capital across continents become a metaphor for an ideal life (to have a lot of money and to enjoy cosmopolitan movement through space) (Morley 2000: 229). Here, an important aspect of this kind of news is that the global dimension of society *is there all the time* in terms of a regular flow of global outlooks on the economy. For the financial elite, the global condition is a rather "normal" dimension of society and an integrated part of life. For the non-elite, on the other hand, who in most cases does not consume this kind of news, the constant news flow of economic figures from the world's stock markets and the related political conversation might cause alienation and give them the feeling that the global world is for someone else (that it is only for the successful class) and/or that this reality is impossible to affect or move in a more democratic direction.

In contrast to "economic global journalism," there is also "extra-economic global journalism." Here, global journalism produces global outlooks on *society as a whole* (not only on business matters). Extra-economic journalism might anchor the abstract global business news in real stories (Moscovici 2001) which go beyond the reifying mechanisms of the market, such as news on the social consequences of the financial meltdown in a small Polish town or how women are affected by it in various parts of the world. Here, one could also include global journalism, involving, for example, environmental, political, technological, or cultural issues. Generally, extra-economic global journalism generates less elite-oriented news and reaches out to wider audiences/users. In some contexts, it might even generate media spectacles and "popular" news discourse (cf. Dahlgren & Sparks 1993) for "mass audiences." Despite the relevance of global crisis reporting (Cottle 2009a), some of it might also be seen as problematic examples of how the news media tends to "dramatize" nuclear threats, financial meltdowns, or various human catastrophes.[6] Despite the fact that global crisis/issue reporting often highlights important relations of peoples and places in the world, emphasizes humanitarianism, and generates charity and political engagement across national borders (Höijer 2004; Chouliaraki 2006), its irregular and thus less integrated way of presenting global processes does not make "global reality" a more natural part of many peoples' lives and understanding of society. As a consequence, for certain elite groups, the global world is a natural part of everyday life, which is partly practiced and symbolized through the consumption of global business news, while for the majority population it still appears to be unreal (abstract flows of global capital) and/or unwanted (a threat to the environment) with only an occasional appearance in the form of particular crises and issues. As a result, the global condition is still not (politically) engaging the majority population in a consistent and fundamental manner.

So how do we make global processes regular and integrated parts of the majority population's "everyday reality"? A neoliberal critic might suggest that economic global journalism ("gj from above") de facto is including rather than excluding people, i.e., that it is intended for *anyone*, not only for some privileged financial elite. The regular flow of stock market discourse from Dow Jones and NASDAQ is, or at least ought to be, everyone's "global language" and reality, and the assumed ideological message would here be "...that human well-being can best be advanced by liberating individual entrepreneurial free-

The Relevance of Global Journalism

doms and skills within an institutional framework characterized by strong private property rights, free markets and free trade" (Harvey 2007: 2). But, here, the spontaneous objection would be that the global world is not merely economics, financial relations, and profit hunting. There is also a global (journalistic) language beyond the global market which needs much more space in the news. In other words, extra-economic global journalism has a crucially important role in which one of the key issues is balancing different global outlooks. If the global outlook is obligatory in the economic news, then it ought to be much more prominent in news on politics and other dimensions of society, too. In the name of journalistic objectivity, then, the global business news discourse needs to be balanced with globally oriented news on political and social thinking, which emanates, not only from the elite but from below (de Sousa Santos 2006).

This is where glopo culture comes into the picture as part of a radical reformation of news journalism. If glopo culture is implemented, news journalism will be able to balance the elite-oriented global economic discourse with another, more democratic type of global news flow, which increases the global empowerment of the majority population. Somewhat paradoxically, then, the basis of the glopo cultural concept is found in the discursive rationale of hardcore economic global journalism, such as in the Dow Jones or Bloomberg global market reporting, but the abstract statistics, charts, and figures are replaced by visible social relations. Imagine that Bloomberg could deliver a vast, *regular flow* of good and bad news about *peoples* and their interconnected lives in a globalizing society from many angles not only from a strictly economic point of view. *Such a global journalism revolution in domestic news media* would popularize and establish the "global village" as a fundamental part of our lives, leaving behind our occasional experiences of (mediated and mediatized) global crises and issues. But at the same time, we need to remember that it is the irregular presence of global news discourse—global crisis reporting and the journalistic focus on various global issues—which pave the way for more glopo culture in the news.

2. More glopo culture is needed in order to reduce the gap between North and South news journalism

The expansion of glopo culture in everyday news might also reduce the narrative divide between the North and South (Jameson 1989). Even if news journalism in many ways looks the same in the economically developed (the North) and developing (the South) parts of the world (cf. de Beer & Merrill 2008) and is shaped by similar mechanisms (Hanitzsch & Mellado 2011), it is still possible to find some important differences in the level of "global consciousness" in discourse, including news journalism.

The North (which is also associated with Western culture) can demonstrate, as described above, rather advanced and sophisticated global journalism when it comes to economic/business news. This could be seen as an expression of the North's continuing economic power in the world (despite recent competition with India and other emerging economic powers) and as a former colonial presence (Klein 2008). The North's historical and continuing material exploitation of the South is thus present in the developed global outlook on money in the news (Carey 1992). One only has to think about the constant flow of stock market news from New York, London or Frankfurt or/and the continuing reporting on how North-based companies expand their markets worldwide (for example, BP, Microsoft or Procter & Gamble). At the same time, as has been suggested, in the case of other types of news (on politics, not least), mainstream news media tend to disconnect global relations (Berglez 2006) for the sake of more narrow domestic and foreign outlooks. In other words, the North (Western) culture and its news journalism tend to repress global narratives by the overproduction of non-global views on political, social, and cultural matters. Several different factors could explain why the advanced global competence in North's economic journalism has not been wholly transferred to other news domains. One potential reason which one should not hesitate to mention is the North's ignorance about the rest of the world (Nederveen Pieterse 2000; Wasserman 2010, 2011a) and/or the conscious as well as unconscious attempt to sweep its responsibility for global welfare and the colonial debt to the South under the carpet (cf. Klein 2008). It is as if too much of politically, socially and culturally oriented global discourse in the everyday news would make the remaining colonial structures too obvious.

In relation to this, it is possible to argue that in the South, glopo culture is more developed than in the North. Fredric Jameson's explanation to this is that

> ...in the centre [First World/the North] there is no need to *know* anything about the periphery [Third World/the South] and therefore, what might become the case is that, when a person in the centre tells the story one does not have to refer to the structures of imperialism and the totality, which means that in these cases, one is excluding from the story how the First World receives its welfare and privileges from the Third World. Epistemologically

speaking, this sort of story could be considered incomplete. (Jameson in Danius & Jonsson 1993: 31. Translated by the author)

And furthermore:

The First World does not need to know about the Third World, while in the Third World, it is rather obvious that it is impossible not to know about the First World. In the periphery, one is aware that living conditions are, in one way or another, determined by absent powers somewhere else. (Jameson in Danius & Jonsson 1993: 31. Translated by the author)

Global journalism's "mission" is to make complex relations visible in the form of news stories, helping us to see how seemingly isolated events, practices, and processes across the world are interconnected. What Jameson seems to argue is that, due to the South's subaltern position (Spivak 1988; Said 1995) in relation to the North, the skill to interconnect the domestic and the global has been refined throughout history, in which "... the colonized mind is parasitically obsessed with the extraneous relation with the colonial powers" (Sen 2007: 89). In the South, then, glopo culture is already well-established and embedded in language and discourse, including news journalism. As a hypothesis, perhaps the most "advanced" kind of global journalism is found in the South.

Needless to say, the global crisis reporting and the focus on important global issues in the North's news media often help to bring less obvious North-South relations to the empirical surface. See Cottle's (2009a) book on global crisis reporting as well as the examples from chapter 2, the climate issue report from Tanzania and the story on H&M's dirty business in Bangladesh. They touch upon problems—"the dark side of globalization" (Cottle 2009a: 22)—which to a great extent are caused by the North: the CO_2 emissions from heavy industry and the systematic exploitation of labor in the developing parts of the world. However, a more pervasive glopo culture in the North's news content would mean that the presence of the South would no longer be limited to particular crises and issues. Instead, news coverage of, for example, living conditions in Kenya and Mali in connection to decisions made in the EU, Sweden, or Great Britain would become much more routine. In other words, a more *consistent flow* of North-South-oriented global journalism, and its establishment of glopo culture, would be able to make radical things happen concerning the narrative divide between the privileged and less privileged parts of the world (Wasserman 2010, 2011a).

GLOBAL JOURNALISM AS A RESPONSE TO THE STATE OF NEWS JOURNALISM

The future of news journalism as a sustainable institution and essential hub for political and democratic processes in society can be more or less taken for granted. Thus, so far, we have not touched upon the debates and research which propose that traditional media institutions no longer represent the natural center of media society (McNair 2005; Couldry 2009; Peters & Broersma 2013) and that journalism has become difficult to define and is undergoing a drastic change in status as a professional practice. Here, some even imply the end of journalism. This is the way in which this argument is usually stated:

> Journalism as it is, is coming to an end. The boundaries between journalism and other forms of public communication—ranging from public relations or advertorials to weblogs and podcasts—are vanishing, the internet makes all other types of news media rather obsolete (especially for young adults and teenagers), commercialization and cross-media mergers have gradually eroded the distinct professional identities of newsrooms and their publications (whether in print or broadcast)... (Deuze 2007: 141)

Deuze (2007) interprets this as part of the emergent "liquid media world." The concept is inspired by Zygmunt Bauman's sociology (2000) and his ideas on the expansion of liquid modernity, which, in turn, seem to build on Marx's classic idea that capitalism is a system where "all that is solid melts into air" (Berman 1983). The liquid state of society means that space, identity, practices, values, etc., become less fixed and determined by tradition and much more individualized. According to this theory, in the media sector old and new concepts converge in ever-new constellations (Jenkins 2006), which also include a collapse of the distinction between professional journalism and other modes of communication. Perhaps, one could define this as the postmodern state of journalism (cf. Jameson 1991); modern journalism's identity as a distinguished practice is challenged by the new postmodern condition in which all kinds of communicative genres tend to converge (journalism, PR, literature, art, research, blogging, etc.).

This way of discussing journalism is further triggered by the long-standing business crisis in the news media sector in some parts of the world, especially among newspapers in the US and Europe (Currah 2009; Hirst 2011). In media and journalism studies, the main driving force behind the "end of journalism," commercially speaking, is assumed to be the technological and digital development of Web 2.0, including social media and user-generated content (UGC). The new digital technology in the context of Internet use has dramatically increased the accessibility of information: ever more information is produced and disseminated via computers and mobile phones, which diminishes traditional news journalism into one voice among many in the public sphere. The uniqueness and exclusiveness of traditional journalistic products are thus assumed to become increasingly weakened. In this new media environment, then, many news companies seem unable to attract the new generations of news consumers (Deuze 2007; Couldry et al. 2006; Currah 2009; Peters & Broersma 2013), who orient themselves to other types of information or produce information themselves in the form of blogs and by means of various social media.

It is often taken for granted that traditional news journalism's crisis is caused *only* by the technological dynamics of the Internet, but perhaps its identity crisis primarily derives from its general inability to renew itself? What if mainstream news media's crisis and expected death are caused by the fact that their journalistic concepts and modes of reporting are too old-fashioned and have become residual?

Among most news companies, technological solutions such as speed, accessibility, quantity, frequency, and immediacy are applied for the sake of continuing commercial attractiveness and competitiveness. However, this might be rather counterproductive. In my view, when "new technology" becomes an essential part of the news brand and product, news producers and professional journalists thus become even *more* vulnerable in comparison, as when it comes to, for example, speed and accessibility, they will always lose out to amateur media, amateur journalists, and the "collective intelligence" of the Web. The sad thing is that too often, the "new technology" seems to be used to mask the lack of new *ideas* on how to narrate today's world in exciting and socially relevant ways (cf. Lovink 2010: 2–3).[7] Thus, news journalism needs to *reinvent* itself: to invent the kinds of journalistic practices and products which cannot be easily surpassed by the 2.0 Web culture and its millions of (mostly non-professional) agents (independent bloggers, UGC, etc.) Or, as Peters & Broersma (2013) put it, journalism needs to be partly *rethought*.

Emergent global journalism, then, could be seen as *one* potential response to the assumed liquid and unsettled state of news journalism and its need for discursive and narrative transformation. By the mid-19th century, the telegraph had established direct lines between London, New Delhi, and New York, but the question still remains as to how journalism could, discursively speaking, better shape the global potential of technology, how could these places become connected in the everyday news in terms of a new, dynamic mode of journalistic storytelling? Such a "communicative revolution" would seem to be a task primarily for professional news journalism. More precisely, then, one could view global journalism as one of several possible "returns" of news journalism as a distinguished professional practice in response to citizen journalism. Ideally, it takes the kind of news which once arose in the national Westphalian order to the next level in close interaction with the entire (global) post-Westphalian condition, including the ever more digitalized and network-oriented dynamics of human information and communication (Castells 1996; Heinrich 2011, 2012) (see chapter 5).

Consequently, the defense of news journalism as a professional practice (and how it could be developed in a global direction) should not be confused with conservatism and the embrace of, for example, Keen's *The Cult of the Amateur* (2007) and its critique of amateur/citizen journalism and social media. The idea is not to neglect the fundamental importance of digital technology for the development of new forms of information and communication beyond traditional news journalism. The point here is that the digital technology revolution does not necessarily generate and promote any revolutionary progress in the art of news reporting and journalistic storytelling (cf. Dahlberg & Snickars 2008). It is quite clear that the contemporary flow of (amateur) digital information is challenging conventional news media in terms of replicating their *traditional* news content and modes of reporting, but it is less clear to what extent it *develops and pushes forward* news journalism as a professional practice. Media technology is wonderful but tomorrow's news journalism will have to build on initiatives which are not merely technology driven but which produce from an increasing number of qualitative and bold ideas creative solutions on how to ever more effectively and attractively incorporate global outlooks in local news reporting.

In order to emphasize the importance of the continued development of news journalism as a distinguished and professional practice, we could compare Google's utopian visions of how to generate and deliver "global knowledge" by means of their gigantic Web archives of information with global journalism as a professional practice. To begin with, Google's chairman, Eric Schmidt, expresses a strong belief in the "collective intelligence" of the Internet in general and Google in particular:

> In the case of individuals, it's the model where the sum of what Google does become the third part of your brain—you know, there's a left brain, a right brain and there's a third part where that collective intelligence that Google can help bring to you really helps you to get through every day: the history of places, what you should do, collecting things for you, telling you what's relevant—the things that computers do best that humans are not good at. And that will leave humans to spend more time doing what humans do best, the things computers are not very good at. I like the emergence of—the marketing buzzword is "collective intelligence," the emergence of the sum of what Facebook, Twitter, Google, the blogging sphere, what is really the beginning of a much deeper understanding of what's really going on in the world. And I find it fascinating that this is what's happening now, and Google is in a position to find it, sort it, rank it, organize it in a way that people who are busy can take advantage of. (Schmidt 2009)

A world without traditional news journalism and news consumption would probably pave the way for an ever more intensified relationship between individual Internet users and the gigantic flow of all kinds of information which is accessible through the efficient search engines of the Web. Currently, Google Search is the master of all available search engines: it redistributes an almost unimaginable number of digital bits, which altogether contribute to a multifaceted picture of what goes on *in* the global village (Ekström 2010; Hillis et al. 2013). In this context, the following comment from Schmidt is interesting: "...collective intelligence,' the emergence of the sum of what Facebook, Twitter, Google, the blogging sphere, what is really the beginning of a much deeper understanding of what's really going on in the world." What he is implying here is that the enormous sum of the information on the Internet might be compatible with the global outlook (the "*deeper* understanding of what's really going on in the world"). The world is viewed as a gigantic puzzle with billions and billions of pieces, and it is assumed that the ever more sophisticated sorting, organizing, and ranking of this information (Google) could give us the ultimate picture of globalizing social reality.

However, technology itself has never been, and will not be, the entire answer to the human development of communication and new forms of knowledge production (Carey 1992). In order to achieve a "deeper understanding of what's really going on in the world" in the near future, professional communicative practices are needed (in the form of news journalism) to "put together" disconnected pieces of information (on events, actions, processes, places, struggles, ideas, etc.) in an illustrative and meaningful manner. Google is only a parasite feeding on existing information, as it does not produce any information itself: its search algorithm and capacity to sort, rank, and organize various pieces of information have no magic ability to present *complex relations* in a globalizing society. This is one of the things that computers (so far) are *not* good at (cf. Harper et al. 2008). Human creativity is required and, in most cases, time, research, professional efforts, and material resources.

I do not claim that global journalism—as a universal concept for news reporting—is the ultimate answer to the problems facing the news business in the present digital revolution, including how to attract new generations of audiences/users. I see it as one among several relevant responses to the rather worn-out (Westphalian) news culture and its continuing lack of a new type of news logic for global times. But of course, here we are facing several important challenges....

4.

Challenges to Global Journalism

This chapter analyzes the main challenges to global journalism. As suggested in Table (4.1), the existing challenges operate mainly at three levels of global journalistic practice. First, they operate at the textual level, which concerns the basic production of global outlooks in journalistic reporting. The second level involves the institutional aspects of global journalism, while the third level concerns its interaction with more general social and cultural processes in society (cf. Fairclough 1995: 57–62).[1]

Consequently, at each and every level one could identify both internal and external challenges. The internal challenges are intimately connected to the very production of global journalism, involving both practical aspects, newsroom decisions, and its status and role in journalism culture as a whole. The external challenges, on the other hand, are less easy to deal with, as they are, to greater extent, beyond the control of those working in a global journalistic direction, involving as they do the general technological development, the preferences and behaviors of news audiences/users, the basic material conditions for producing journalism, and so forth. Below, I will focus on a number of challenges which operate primarily at one particular level, but it is important to note that these could interact with internal and external challenges at the other levels as well.

Cognitive and discursive challenges. More or less intertwined, these are primarily associated with the textual level. But, these challenges, which involve the basic practice of global journalism communication, are definitely in a dialectical relationship with overall media institutional factors (journalistic routines, policies, editorial traditions, etc.) as well as with overall social and cultural processes.

Table 4.1. Various Challenges to Global Journalism

Challenges level	Internal challenges	External challenges
At the textual level	• The management of producing journalism with global outlooks (i.e., its cognitive and discursive challenges)	• Its development and position in relation to other news modes, be it local reporting, foreign news, or hyperlocal information • Its development in relation to various media technological and news discursive processes, such as the impact of social media, mobile phone communication and news apps)
At the institutional level	• Its professional and commercial development in small as well as bigger media organizations and newsrooms • Its development in relation to existing material and technological resources at the particular media company or media hub • Its position and role in the context of journalism training	• Its ability to function in diverse institutional contexts, i.e., among various groups of news audiences/users and consumers • Its ability to become adopted by a new generation of media practitioners (journalists, editors, journalism students, etc.)
At the overall social and/or cultural level	• Its ability to interact and integrate with entire journalism cultures within nation-states as well as in the world • Its future position in the overall "media culture," and ability to expand in the entire news market	• Its ability to adapt to and/or overcome particular structural conditions in society, be they material, historical, ideological, material, or technological ones (for example, the possible lack of basic digital and technological infrastructure in a country)

Professional challenges. The development of global journalism as a professional practice and identity is primarily associated with the institutional level (for example, its development among the staff in a media company and/or newsroom environment), while it dynamically interacts and/or conflicts with challenges at the textual level (its development as a mode of reporting) as well as at the social/cultural level (for example, its status in the broader journalism culture).

Commercial challenges. The challenge of making global journalism more commercially sustainable is primarily associated with the institutional level (editorial practices and decisions, etc.). However, it also includes particular strategies at the textual level (on how to actually do the global journalistic "packeting" of news in relation to other types of journalism and news reporting) as well as at the overall social/cultural level to make global journalism a more natural part of media culture and the entire news business.

Ideological challenges. This concerns global journalism's ability to balance the principles of objectivity with the promotion and/or repression of various ideological ideas and interests. This challenge is primarily associated with the social/cultural level, as it involves global journalism's interplay with pervasive ideas in society and their ideological consequences. However, the presence or absence of this or that ideology in global journalistic reporting is intertwined with journalistic and editorial practices at the textual and institutional levels.

Material and technological challenges. These challenges, often intertwined, could be present both at the institutional and social/cultural level. Furthermore, the material resources in a media company (the institutional level) as well as in a particular country (the social/cultural level) influence and involve the textual level, i.e., the basic practice of global journalism.

Educational challenges. These challenges are primarily associated with activities at the institutional level in terms of journalism education and training. However, training involves challenges at the text level (practical methods) as well as at the social/cultural level (could further training transform existing journalism cultures?).

COGNITIVE AND DISCURSIVE CHALLENGES

Global journalism involves complex relationships between "...cognition, society and discourse" (van Dijk 1998: 5). Cognition refers to the underlying mental frameworks in human communication, involving memory, beliefs and ideas. Discourse, on the other hand, concerns the actual language use. Cognition and discourse operate at the individual level as well as culturally and socially speaking, i.e., at the socio-cognitive and socio-cultural level of communication (Moscovici 1996, 2001). In this respect, from a cognitive point of view, a global outlook on society could be described as a schema and "...a mental structure which contains general expectations and knowledge of the world" (Augoustinos & Walker 1996: 33), which dialectically interacts with the discursive production of such an outlook (i.e., the meaning-making and the very use of language). In the news media, numerous events constantly need to be explained by means of a global outlook, but a particular cognitive and discursive barrier in news journalism prevents this from happening. The barrier is the fact that, in comparison to the national outlook, the global outlook is not well enough established either among journalists or among the news audiences/users (as socio-cognition and socio-culture). Thus, the overall friction between global reality and mainstream news journalism is basically *a cognitive and discursive problem* in the sense that news journalism still relies too much on the kind of pre-global cognition and discourse which were firmly established in the past.

In the present era of liquid modernity (Bauman 2000; Deuze 2007) *multitasking* has become a widespread buzzword and a desirable skill in many professional contexts. So far, its breakthrough in the field of media production has evolved around the technical and digital ability to combine several media platforms simultaneously in the name of media convergence (Jenkins 2006). However, what is still missing is the advanced skill of cognitively and discursively managing multiple spaces, powers, and identities (local, national, regional, international, transnational and global) simultaneously in the construction of news stories.

Thus, the great challenge for those who argue for the need to expand the presence of global journalism in everyday news is to change the dominant mindscape. Most media owners, editors, and journalists do not primarily expect the world to be globally complex but concentrate instead on local and/or national factors, as do most news audiences/users. Due to their mutual (socio-cognitive and socio-cultural) reproduction of traditional domestic and foreign outlooks on social reality, both media producers and audiences/users tend to "immediately" identify and interpret events or actions as "purely" national or "purely" foreign and thereby neglect the potential transnational or global dimension which might be buried under the discursive surface (see Olausson 2005; Östman 2009). We might want to ask whether a certain event/phenomenon/issue was solely "Swedish." Or solely "Turkish." Or "Hungarian."

As has already been mentioned, contemporary news journalism has developed in parallel with the modern nation-state and its institutions, and, therefore, today's cognitive schemas are rather sluggish and hard to transform in a more transnational direction. According to Billig's (1995), Anderson's (1991), van Dijk's (1988) research conclusions, the strong national outlook on reality is based on a constant interplay between certain cognitive structures (national memory, national borders, and so forth), and discourse, such as the constant naming of things as national (the weather, places, events, you name it). This makes it so difficult to leave behind the limited focus on the local place, home nation, or foreign event and to instead develop new *routines* which smoothly insert/embed the surrounding world in the regular news reporting of local, national, and foreign affairs.

What makes the cognitive and discursive challenge so demanding is the ideological power of the traditional local and national outlooks. They have turned into the most basic and natural kinds of representations (van Dijk 1998: 8), so that it might seem quite difficult to think outside and beyond them (cf. Berglez 2011a). In the journalistic routines (research, collection of sources, fact-checking, interviewing, reporting, etc.) to make the home nation an overall frame for the story is considered easy work, or more likely, it is in most cases just taken for granted. It's the basics. For example, for a Swedish journalist, it seems the most natural thing in the world to frame society as "Sweden," i.e., as synonymous with the nation-state of Sweden.

But, objectively speaking, is it more difficult to include a global outlook on news reporting than, for example, a traditional national one? The spontaneous answer to this ought to be "yes, of course, this is a trickier task." But on the other hand, we need to remember that although the national outlook is *nowadays* seen as "easy work," in the early days of the (Westphalian) nation-state it was perceived as a more demanding kind of practice. Back then, the national outlook required *creative inventions of routines*. And back then, it represented a *particular* new idea and political goal among particular powers and groups who were striving for the expansion of a nation-state, and therefore it was *introduced* into various discourses (often in the form of nationalism), including media and journalism (cf. Rantanen 2009; Anderson 1991). Gradually, due to the development of the entire international system of nation-states it became a *universal* feature of journalistic language. In present times, the particular news style of global journalism might seem superfluous as well as too complex or alien to some media practitioners and news audiences/users. But provided that cognitive and discursive barriers are gradually geared towards the global, "globalizing routines" in news production will gradually turn it into "normal routines" and thereby become a more *universal* and taken-for-granted ingredient.

On territories and borders

Perhaps one drastic cognitive and discursive solution would be to tear down all borders in news journalism's representations of social reality. In order to emphasize the existence of a singular, common, global world or community (Ibold & Kioko 2012), should one not cover global crises and issues in a *radically borderless mode* by, as far as possible, avoiding mentioning particular local places, nations, regions, or continents? This is probably a bad idea, as this kind of reporting would be unable to connect to basic news values (Galtung & Ruge 1965) such as meaning and relevance. After all, one cannot wink at the fact that the world is divided into different territories. For example, climate change is a truly global process, but climate reporting still "needs" to discuss particular nations and local places, events, actions, or cultures in order to deliver meaningful information (cf. Moscovici 2001: 42). Consequently, borders, both the "real" and the imagined ones, are fundamental aspects of human cognition and discourse (the inside/outside, here/there), and it is hard to imagine a society or world without them. Society is based on language, while language, including the language of journalism, is synonymous with the production of differences and a system of differences (Derrida 1978; Berglez 1997). A could not exist without B and C, and in accordance with a similar rationale, there is no global dimension or space (material/physical) to speak of (to cognitively and discursively represent) without the national territory or the local place.

To put this in another way: it is not the constant referring to territorial borders (local, national, etc.) which acts a barrier to the development of global journalism but the ways in which borders are usually applied in mainstream news journalism. In this context, it is relevant to distinguish between *border-determined journalism* and *border-reflexive journalism*. The great challenge is to accomplish a relative shift from the first to the second.

Border-determined journalism Border-reflexive journalism

Traditionally, in journalism, the place where an event takes place ("happens") tends to colonize the entire story: it steers the background information, selection of sources, themes, verbal comments and reactions, the overall context, the representation of identity, power, and so forth (cf. van Dijk 1988: 55). This is border-determined journalism, a serious barrier to global journalism which future generations of journalists need to overcome. Border-reflexive journalism, on the other hand, establishes more playful and even unpredictable modes of handling space and territorial borders. A reported event from, for example, Madrid, covered by Spanish or Swedish media, is not pre-determined and limited to local or national borders, that is, by the "place" Madrid or Spain, as the story's contextual information, verbal comments, cause and effect reasoning, etc. build on interconnections with other territories and places. A reporter covers an event in "A" by simultaneously referring to places, processes, and reactions outside of "A." We need to imagine the kind of complex social relationships which the World Wide Web tends to constitute across territories and between spaces (in the case of transnational cybercrime, etc.) and the new journalistic competence required for covering and investigating such matters.

The requested spatial flexibility in news journalism occasionally appears in, for example, the reporting of terrorism, as the activities of terrorist networks often involve several places simultaneously (certainly true in the case of 9/11). The cognitive and discursive power and dominance of border-determined journalism make it difficult to apply such a reporting rationale where the global interrelations between spaces are less obvious. However, a climate reporter whom I interviewed some years ago shows the way by sharing another example of a "border-progressive" journalism:

> [Concerning climate change].... I think it is very old-fashioned to talk about domestic *or* foreign news, to me this does not exist. But for me, it is more like, this happens in a city in Holland, and this appears somewhere else, and let us interrelate these events in the coverage. I have always done this...worked thematically. (Berglez 2011a: 461)

Even though this is an essential aspect of the future of journalism, I realize that it can only expand and develop to a certain degree. The journalistic and editorial routine of reducing the media event to the place where it obviously "happens" is a deeply naturalized practice and expresses a fundamental aspect of human cognition which is hard to displace entirely. Of course, the news reporting on an accident in a particular country necessarily "needs" descriptions and sources such as eyewitnesses which are physically and materially bound to the place where the accident "happens." In other words, border-reflexive journalism should never completely replace border-determined journalism, but it has an important role to play.

On the domestic and foreign, the proximate and the distant

The above discussion on borders points to the fact that global journalism is, by definition, an attempt to challenge the tradition in news journalism of making a sharp cognitive and discursive distinction between the *proximate* (the domestic world) and the *distant* (the foreign world). What is "here" and is happening "here" constitute domestic news, and what is "there" and is happening over "there" constitute foreign news. Thus, as a consequence, the great global journalistic "mission" is to intensify the cognitive and discursive movement which moves from the left to the right in Table 4.2 and to turn this into a natural routine.

Table 4.2. The Cognitive and Discursive Handling of the Proximate and Distant in Global Journalism

To journalistically detect the:	in the:	and thereby:
geographically, culturally, politically, and socially *distant*	geographically, culturally, politically, and socially *proximate*	"foreignize" the domestic
geographically, culturally, politically, and socially *proximate*	geographically, culturally, politically, and socially *distant*	"domesticize" the foreign

Consequently, there are numerous relations between "here" and "there" which are invisible and never reach the news because they presuppose cognitive and discursive routines which are too much outside the traditional rationale of news media production and media logic (cf. Berglez 2011a). More precisely, then, the effort to make these relations visible presupposes hard journalistic labor in terms of objectifications. In accordance with Moscovici's sociocognitive theoretical reasoning:

> Objectification saturates the idea of unfamiliarity with reality, turns it into the very essence of reality. Perceived at first in a purely intellectual, remote universe, it then appears before our eyes, physical and accessible. (Moscovici 2001: 49)

In media which only occasionally produce *objectifications of the global*, global reality is continually primarily associated with "...unfamiliar and abstract notions, ideas and images... [and not] ... concrete and objective common-sense realities" (Augoustinos & Walker 1996: 139). The only kind of journalism which is "allowed" to constantly deliver abstract global information without objectifying it (i.e., making it concrete) is financial/economic news journalism. The image of the global economy as an abstract and distant force (figures, statistics, transnational processes without visible and identifiable agents, etc.) instead of concrete and "humanized" relationships between peoples and their various practices is somehow culturally accepted (see also the discussion below on ideological challenges). But, for other types of global information, objectifications are of fundamental importance from a news value perspective, i.e., to make the global dimensions of social reality as concrete and proximate as possible. As a consequence, an important challenge is to learn how to *anchor* global processes in the already familiar, be it in already established types of journalism, spaces, cultures, traditions, ideas, etc. Again, we need to immerse ourselves in Serge Moscovici's socio-cognitive theory:

> [Anchoring] ...is a process which draws something foreign and disturbing [global reality] that intrigues us into our particular system of categories and compares it to the paradigm of a category which we think to be suitable.... To anchor is thus to classify and to name something. Things that are unclassified and unnamed are alien, non-existent and at the same time threatening. We experience a resistance, a distancing when we are unable to evaluate something, to describe it to ourselves or to other people. The first step towards overcoming such resistance, towards conciliating an object or person, is taken when we are able to place it or him in a given category, to label it or him with a familiar name. Once we can speak about something, assess it and thus communicate it—even vaguely, as when we say of someone that he is "inhibited"—then we can represent the unusual in our usual world, reproduce it as a replica of a familiar model. By classifying what is unclassifiable, naming what is unnamable, we are able to imagine it, to represent it. (Moscovici 2001: 42)

To begin with, (disturbing) relations are repressed by the news, as they do not have a name (they are neither entirely domestic or foreign), but global journalism is the mode of reporting which takes on the challenge to utter their name (i.e., global relations) and to anchor them in already familiar and established cognition (in the domestic, or foreign ways of comprehending social reality). The end goal of this challenge would then be to utter "global relations" in news reporting so many times that they gradually no longer have to be constantly voiced, to the extent that they become naturalized (taken for granted) as a way of looking at social reality.

On introvert and extrovert domestications

A possible objection to Table 4.2 might be that "domestication of foreign events" is already a full-fledged practice among the world's domestic media. Here, the argument would be that—as demonstrated in Galtung & Ruge's (1965) classic study on news values—domestic media actually prioritize the kind of foreign reporting which manages to include some domestic angle. For example, Swedish foreign reporting usually tends to emphasize such questions as "Are any Swedes involved?" "What will Sweden do?" and so forth. The domestic interests might even colonize the foreign coverage. Even if the report is supposed to primarily focus on "them" and "their" country, event, or problem, it might soon degenerate into coverage about "us" and the way in which "we" are involved or affected and thereby become a serious barrier to global and cosmopolitan modes of journalism (Riegert 1998, 2009, 2011). Thus, in this context it is important to distinguish between *introvert* and *extrovert* domestications in news journalism. It is true that introvert domestications are serious barriers to global journalism. An extrovert domestication, on the other hand, is a routine which should be considered an essential part of global journalism, as it aims to establish an *interconnection* of some kind (social, ethical, cultural, or political) between the foreign worlds/conditions and the domestic world.

INTROVERT DOMESTICATIONS → ITS "WE" <u>AND</u> THE WORLD
OR "WE" <u>OR</u> THE WORLD

EXTROVERT DOMESTICATIONS → ITS "WE" <u>IN</u> THE WORLD
OR "WE" <u>IN RELATION TO</u> THE WORLD

In other words, introvert domestications emphasize the imagined abyss or distance between the "we" and the surrounding world, while extrovert domestications seek to reduce that distance. The challenge, then, is to expand the use of extrovert domestications at the expense of the introvert ones.

On cultural and relational proximity in news journalism

Introvert and extrovert domestications touch upon the conflict between *cultural proximity* and *relational proximity* in which global journalism represents the seemingly naïve but nevertheless necessary attempt to push relational proximity forward (see also chapter 2). Cultural proximity in journalism revolves around the common identity (Olausson 2009a), which is predominately of the local and/or national kind, based on the common language, ethnicity, ideology, or religion and characterized by the domestic "us" in ways which primarily reproduce cultural status quo. Practices of relational proximity, on the other hand, make the seemingly distant, foreign world more prominent in the domestic world and vice versa (see Table 4.2), thereby paving the way for cultural transformation (Berglez & Olausson 2011). For example, if Swedish media would radically increase news on EU affairs and how Brussels influences Sweden and the lives of Swedish citizens, this would probably, in the long term, transform the Swedish political culture into a more EUropean one (Berglez 2007; Olausson 2010). Consequently, in the case of relational proximity, journalism links local and national affairs with the surrounding world and thereby brings new and "external" light on the internal/domestic cultural traditions and "ways of life" (i.e., "we" are a culture but "we" seem to be very interconnected with the world).

However, cultural proximity and relational proximity are not two separate cognitive and discursive practices; their relationship is dialectical. Journalism driven by relational proximity still presupposes cultural proximity (i.e., traditional domestications). For example, a news story in the local paper in the Swedish city of Örebro, which focuses on the emerging global problem of antibiotic resistance and includes domestications in terms of paying attention to how it affects the Örebro region, simply needs to be anchored in the cultural "us" (the local citizens of Örebro) in order to attract the attention of local news audiences/users. However, if cultural proximity is *combined* with relational proximity, the coverage does not entirely "collapse" into introvert domestications but instead stimulates reflexive thinking on how to conceive the relation between the proximate and distant, that is, the "here" and "there" (spatially, politically, socially, ecologically, etc.). And at the cultural level, it is possible to assume that the flourishing of relational proximity paves the way for a transnational transformation of the notion of "us" (Berglez & Olausson 2011; Polson & Kahle 2010). Here, then, the great challenge is to pave the way for global journalism by establishing a functional balance between cultural and relational proximity.

PROFESSIONAL CHALLENGES

So far, this book has presented examples of global journalism (chapter 2) as well as ideas on its relevance for mainstream news (chapter 3). However, we need to take into account the challenges to its professional breakthrough in news production and news usage/consumption.

The global journalist as the ultimate foreign reporter

In order to pave the way for the professional status of global journalism, one important challenge is to resolve the confusion as to what global journalism is as well as what it ought to be (cf. Berglez 2008). Here, the idea is not to suppress animated discussion on the conceptual essence of global journalism (this book suggests one particular definition and vision but there are others as well: see chapter 1). However, I have noticed that, when discussing this book's definition of global journalism to various audiences, its practice often becomes associated with the work of the traditional foreign reporter, or more precisely, too quickly it becomes categorized as "foreign journalism in global times." At least, there is one understandable rationale for this. Together, the two words "Global" and "journalism" connote "international affairs" and news information from distant places, elements which remind us of traditional foreign reporting. The problem, then, is that this rationale paves the way for the impression that global journalism does not presuppose some change in journalism or contribute a fresh perspective on news production ("Is not this simply traditional foreign reporting in a new disguise?"). Further discussions are needed about how global journalism actually represents a new kind of professional competence which is breaking with foreign reporting's way of enhancing the world but without neglecting the continuing relevance of traditional foreign news in many contexts.

Furthermore, due to this conceptual confusion, global journalism also becomes associated with prestigious foreign news scoops and risk taking by correspondents in dangerous places in the world. It might be confused with professional "globetrotting," i.e., constant movement from one place to another, from one crisis region or conflict to another. Perhaps, in some circles, the global journalist is imagined as a nomadic and cosmopolitan subject who smoothly transports her-/himself from one continent to another.

The association with foreign correspondence might then partly explain why few journalists would consider themselves as skilled in the art of global journalism. (Another reason, which is probably even more important, is that global journalism is still mainly an academic concept, and thus the term seldom used by media practitioners.)

However, many media practitioners who are not foreign correspondents should become aware of the fact that they de facto practice something called global journalism, perhaps without knowing it. Certainly, the traditional field work of foreign correspondents, to actually visit and report from foreign places, improves one's ability to deliver global outlooks, but my point is that the global journalist might as well be seen as an "ordinary" journalist who works from a domestic (local/national) platform and captures global interconnections in his/her reporting by means of his/her global knowledge, social media sources, journalistic network (Heinrich 2011, 2012) and connections around the world, etc. (cf. Beckett 2010). "Think globally, act locally" is a worn-out and banal buzzword, but journalists still need to be conscious in these global times that they must act from where they are standing.

Global journalism as a unique skill/talent or a basic routine in the editorial room and in the field?

So far, this book has only briefly touched upon the question of whether or not global journalism could and should develop as a particular niche among a few experts or into a basic routine among editors and journalists. In my view, the goal to aim for is the latter. However, it is clear that there is a potential conflict between the two alternatives. If global journalism remains a skill which only a minority of journalists are supposed to be familiar with, in terms of being one man's job in the newsroom and/or editorial office, then this will likely hinder the breakthrough of global journalism among journalists in general, including the expansion of global outlooks on all kinds of news issues and topics.

Here, a more basic problem, I would say, is that, too often, quality in journalism, including future journalism, is discussed in terms of individual gifts rather than as the development of particular methods and routines. This could to great extent be explained by the fact that the journalism sector, like most other sectors, has a star system which revolves around personalities and their supposedly unique talents. I recently participated at a UK conference in the UK in which the panel discussants (both academics and practitioners) almost exclusively discussed the issue of quality in journalism by referring to particular columnists, investigative reporters, or foreign correspondents and their extraordinary columns, interview techniques, reflections on society, etc. in elite media such as *The Independent* and *The Times*. Too much emphasis on the assumed "genius" or talent of particular individuals tends to send the signal that their skills are difficult and too complicated to translate to the "ordinary reporter" in any editorial organization. The highlighted journalistic skills somehow become mystified rather than democratized. I do not want to ignore the fact that "celebrity journalists" and role models might be important for the development of new styles and routines, including global journalism. In Sweden, the weekly news program *Korrespondenterna* (The Correspondents) on Sweden's Public Service Television, which brings together some of the best and most experienced editors and journalists in the country, continually demonstrates rather impressive examples of global journalism. But still, what is really important is to take advantage of such (embryonic) and exemplary cases and transform them into accessible routines which could be applied among journalists and editors.

COMMERCIAL CHALLENGES

This book focuses on the potential development of global journalism in traditional news media, but it is possible to imagine its expansion in other media contexts as well—in independent media, among citizen journalists, and in the blogosphere. However, no matter where it might potentially develop and even flourish, and irrespective of the size and character of the media organization, development will likely generate costs. Therefore, it needs some kind of market-driven business model or alternative financing such as the public service model in which the funding is guaranteed by a public license fee (Collins 2011). The present liquid state of traditional journalism (Deuze 2007, 2011) calls for a revitalization of news and new ideas, and even a paradigm shift in news journalism, and thereby supposedly "...experimentation with new forms of media is growing" (Kurpius et al. 2010: 360). Ideally, in this context, global journalism should be seen as a fresh kind of news information which is endowed with some commercial potential, but, due to certain conditions and factors it is likely to be associated with commercial barriers and thus serious challenges.

The most basic barrier is the overall fiscal crisis in the news business in large parts of the world (Picard 2008), involving the newspaper industry in particular. In the US (Downie & Schudson 2009) as well as in several European countries such as in the UK (Currah 2009; Collins 2011) and Sweden (Berglez 2010) the news audiences/users are tending to abandon traditional news media for other sources of information and media platforms, particularly for the Web and mobile communication. Those newspapers which have fully adopted the Web and the digitalization of journalism may still have a large readership but the problem is their decreased ability to generate enough advertising revenue (Kurpius et al. 2010: 360). Advertising strategies have become more complex and advanced in a constantly changing Web landscape in which consumers' and users' behaviors are difficult to follow and predict. "Whatever the future of journalism, much of it depends on understanding the ways that people navigate the digital news environment—the behavior of what might be called the new news consumer" (Olmstead et al. 2011: 1). The financing problems might then also negatively affect the quality of news information, in which too "expensive" journalism is replaced by PR materials (Reich 2010), notes from news agencies, stories based solely on secondhand sources and material, etc. (Currah 2009).

On hyperlocal news

Besides the overall business crisis, there is an additional commercial barrier to global journalism that concerns the power of the local. More precisely, the ongoing discussion of new business models is not primarily focusing on global aspects of journalism but rather on hyperlocal news. In other words, the recent trend has been to further explore and exploit our inbuilt request for geographically and culturally proximate information:

> Hyperlocal media operations are geographically-based news organizations that operate largely in big metropolitan areas and cover a range of location-specific topics. Such sites allow input from citizens through content contribution, blogs, and other feedback loops. In the current media environment, hyperlocal media operate at the crossroads of highly focused, locally-oriented news with technology-enabled potentials as tools for civic engagement. (Kurpius et al. 2010: 360; see also Metzgar et al. 2011)

This is a mode of producing news which thus seeks to be even more local than traditional local news and in which contributions from citizens (citizen journalism) play an important role (Jarvis 2009; Metzgar et al. 2011). In numerous "future of journalism" blogs, lists, and discussions, it is constantly repeated that the future news consumer will request more personally relevant news in which the local community is supposed to be a central component.

The conceptual confusion between global journalism and (the expensive) traditional foreign reporting probably makes it seem somewhat stupid or at least like very bad timing to imagine a commercial expansion of global journalism. How could one even dare to dream about developed forms of global journalism on the media market in times of a serious crisis for news production and journalism which has caused the dismantling of numerous foreign offices and reporters (Currah 2009)? Under such conditions, of course, it might seem more natural and rational to focus on the commercial potentials of the local or even hyperlocal kind of information.

However, so far, despite the hyped status of hyperlocal news in certain media circles and its association with the future of journalism, it has been hard to make it profitable; in the US most hyperlocal media companies are unable to establish an advertising-driven business model (Kurpius et al. 2010: 373). The increasing importance and popularity of social media as a source of personal information and communication might help to explain the fact that, so far, hyperlocal news is hardly a commercial success story. The point is that, if the news become *too* hyperlocal, such as, to take an extreme example, news on the neighbor's cat's mysterious disappearance, it will likely become outcompeted by other sources of information and communication such as various social media sites and community networks. In other words, the media industry could only "exploit" our inbuilt desire for hyperlocal information so far.

In some sense, it is understandable that in a complex reality, many of us would like to flee into a smaller world. This is what Bauman (1995) and other sociologists have described as a natural consequence of globalization. But I find it strange that so many of the discussions on "the future of journalism" and its supposedly creative and innovative activities retreat into that small world as well by focusing on the hyperlocal (see Jarvis 2009). It is quite difficult to find interesting projects that seek to take on the challenge of developing commercially sustainable models for dynamically merging the local and the global. More news business initiatives are certainly needed which, via various media platforms and modes of discourse (textually, verbally, visually, and audiovisually), aim to develop and refine the kind of domestic news information that integrates the global in its content. It is reasonable to assume that, due to our inbuilt conservatism as news consumers/users, a serious commercial development of global news discourse could only become realized by linking global journalistic ambitions and creativity with the "natural" interest in the domestic (local as well as national events, concerns, interests, etc.). However, I hope that the result would be ever new, smart, and relevant forms of local and/or national news discourse which do not simply move inward, that is, towards the hyperlocal and "thick" community but outward to the inescapable globalizing *society*.

But what about public service broadcasting?

At least hypothetically, more bold attempts to globalize journalism and the news ought to be possible in public service broadcasting organizations, as these tend to have a more stable income. But here we need to take account of two things. First, one needs to remember that public service media companies operate under national regulations and on behalf of the particular nation-state, which means that their media content is dominated by the traditional national outlook on society and a foreign outlook on the world. In other words, public service broadcasting companies do not necessarily provide their audiences/users with more global kinds of news than commercial media (i.e., there is still much to develop in this area: see Berglez 2010). Second, the public service concept is rather marginalized and/or questioned in many countries (Collins 2002, 2011), and more recently even in countries with a strong tradition of public service broadcasting, such as the UK and the Scandinavian countries. When it comes to the particular case of Europe, in the 1980s and 1990s the EU began to put pressure on the member nation-states to de-regulate their national media systems (Collins 2002; Syvertsen 2003; Bardoel & d'Haenens 2008). In this context, the EU's intention was to reduce the assumed privileges and power of national public service broadcasting companies by paving the way for further "liberation" of the media market in the name of more equal and free competition. However, the marketization of the national media sectors, a process driven by the EU but also by other factors and interests, has hardly contributed to further media pluralism and diversity and thus to more "globally complex news discourse," at least not in countries such as Sweden. Instead, it has established a condition of media concentration in which a few actors are controlling more and more of the total media market and its various channels (television, radio, newspapers including various digital services) (cf. Moe 2008), with a homogenization of media content as an apparent consequence. It is possible to assume that the increasing demand among public service companies to compete with the private media sector will hardly allow for loads of creativity and risky development projects in the area of news production but will rather lead to further adaptation to the market logic.

MATERIAL AND TECHNOLOGICAL CHALLENGES

The material and technological challenges to global journalism are quite intertwined. Here, it seems natural to pay attention to the basic material divide between the Global North (developed countries) and Global South (developing countries). It is a structural condition which negatively affects the latter's ability to invest in needed technological infrastructure for public communication, including news production and journalism. In developing countries, access to technological resources and infrastructure is essential if media are to contribute to development of communication (Waisbord 2005), i.e., to democratic processes and participation as well as to the overall social development, including material/economic growth.

Material and technological challenges might involve scarce or apparent lack of economic resources in terms of competent staff, premises, transportation, computers, mobile phones, cameras, and video equipment as well as deficient mobile phone, radio, or cable systems, and/or lack of broadband access and speed. Some technological barriers might involve the relationship of the media system and the political system (Hallin & Mancini 2004) and more precisely certain political/governmental barriers and the lack of democratic infrastructure. For example, the lack of access to some technological infrastructure might be explained by restrictions of press freedom and freedom of speech (cf. Al-Saqaf 2010).

Despite the fact that they were formulated more than 30 years ago, the central recommendations of the MacBride Report (UNESCO 1980) are still extremely important. In many developing countries, problems such as lack of communications infrastructure, and the need for improved conditions for journalists and other media practitioners have only just been solved if they have actually been solved (cf. Balnaves et al. 2009: 155). In the wake of the MacBride Report, political and economic research on the technological barriers to media production and journalism in general has to a great extent focused on information and communication technologies (ICTs). The North-South issue has been conceptualized in terms of a digital divide (Norris 2001) and has been analyzed as a natural extension of traditional colonialism, i.e., as electronic colonialism (McPhail 1987, 2010) in which the Global North's vast advantage in ICTs is supposed to maintain and even increase the basic material inequalities in the world. However, there are also some positive developments to be mentioned such as the mobile phone boom in many developing countries. Provided that journalism and new methods for production and distribution of news information will continue to develop in relation to the increasing mobile phone traffic in the Global South, it might become possible to radically reduce some of the barriers just mentioned (Etzo & Collender 2010; Wasserman 2011b).

Concerning technological barriers/challenges to the particular practice of global journalism, it is possible to reflect upon the extent that global outlooks

Challenges to Global Journalism

in news reporting are de facto dependent on advanced technical solutions. Naturally, global journalistic work is dependent on access to technical equipment such as, for example, a tape recorder or a video cam as well as such technological infrastructure as a computer with decent Internet connectivity and speed that makes it possible to access Web sources or databases in actual investigative work. However, despite what has just been said about the fundamental importance of technical means, we still need to remember that what *basically* constitutes global journalism is the epistemological component. Its practice is primarily based on a global mode of thinking about society (cognition) and global language use (discourse). Consequently, despite the fact that it could be developed by various digital solutions (for example, see my modest attempt in chapter 5), its foundation is simply the aim to identify relevant relations across nations and continents, which can be done without any of the latest digital technology. Advanced technological means might support and streamline the global journalistic mode of reporting, but they could never *replace* its basic epistemological routines and practices.

IDEOLOGICAL CHALLENGES

News journalism, including global journalism, might become ideologically oriented and thus partisan in terms of promoting certain values and interests which speak to members of a group, thereby establishing a socio-cultural alliance between the producers and consumers/users of the news information. Ideological elements in news journalism are inevitable and in many cases rather necessary as social reality itself is not neutral. Despite the fundamental importance of the objectivity principle (Westerståhl 1983; Berglez 2003), often it is necessary for journalists to take an ideological stand for an interest, a group, or a political struggle for the sake of democracy, freedom or justice (cf. partisan journalism or advocacy journalism). What particularly characterizes the relationship of global journalism and ideology and what potential pitfalls can we imagine? Here, the challenge is to develop a global journalism which is able to establish a proper balance between ideological engagement and the principles of objectivity (balance and pertinence). In this context, then, we need to pay attention not only to the extra-economic kind of global journalism (which is our main analytical concern in this book) but also to economic global journalism or global business news) and their rather contrasting ideological dynamics and functions (see also chapter 3). Here, the assumption is that too much ideology in global journalistic reporting might work against its ability to develop into a basic and universal routine in the context of mainstream media production. The practices of traditional local or foreign reporting are not immediately associated with any particular ideology (for example, foreign news reporting could interplay with Leftist as well as Rightist worldviews), and this is what makes these modes of reporting universal in the field of news production. Global journalism ought to adopt the same attitude.

The very concept of ideology, then, is quite complex and could be defined in various ways (Thompson 1990). In this context, I primarily lean toward a sociopsychological definition in which ideology is seen as a particular way of cognitively and discursively structuring society within a group (van Dijk 1998):

> In that framework, ideologies may be very succinctly defined as the basis of the social representations shared by members of a group. This means that ideologies allow people, as group members, to organize the multitude of social beliefs about what is the case, good or bad, right or wrong, for them, and to act accordingly. (van Dijk 1998: 8)

However, in order to link ideology to its Marxist and critical theoretical heritage (Thompson 1990), it is important to emphasize that ideological discourse by necessity includes elements of power, interests and values.

Extra-economic global journalism and ideology

In the case of extra-economic global journalism, which, in contrast to global business news, delivers global outlooks of the social, political, cultural, environmental, etc., kinds, we ought to pay attention to its ability to deliver the "bigger picture" on the negative consequences of economic globalization. An important aspect here is its potential to embed the covered events in identified global processes, crises/threats, or issues, such as the nuclear threat, climate change, market capitalism, or the overall energy or food crisis in the world. It is a mode of reporting which thus often stimulates the global side of citizenship and democratic engagement in terms of questioning, and discursively challenging, global powers and interests. As has been demonstrated in previous chapters, the extra-economic kind of global journalism tends to conceptualize poverty and social inequalities, not as self-inflicted concerns/problems in particular regions or parts of the world but instead as a *structural* problem which involves the globe as a *totality*, i.e., the relation between the Global North and the Global South. In other words, the extra-economic kind of global journalism often interplays with the "globalization-from-below" kind of thinking (Callero 2008; Berglez 2011b).

What I am getting at is that this variant of global journalism often seems to interplay with basic Leftist thinking and more precisely the critique of ideology, i.e., the intellectual attempt to unmask hidden power structures (Althusser 2001). Thus, in Western market capitalist societies, Leftist/Marxist thinking tends to deliver counter-hegemonic discourse by bringing up to the surface a global context and social totality (i.e., the destructive effects of global capitalism) (Jameson 1991) and by letting it work as a master explanation of the world's problems (the climate, energy issue, the nuclear weapon threat, the digital divide, etc.).

On the one hand, this kind of "Leftist global journalism" is much needed from a democratic point of view as it covers the global world "from below." On the other hand, what is less requested is the development of a (propagandistic) Leftist global journalistic practice which is somehow preset to, no matter what topic is at stake, put the blame on global market capitalism and its assumed interests, again and again, and thereby turns into an extremely predictable kind of news reporting, ideologically speaking.

The above reasoning paves the way for the idea that extra-economic global journalism should be seen as a rather Leftist mode of reporting. Extra-economic global journalism does not, however, automatically generate Leftist and/or counter-hegemonic world views. It is, of course, possible to imagine, for example, global crisis reporting which is rather balanced and ideologically complex. And we need to remember that extra-economic global journalism might as well interplay with hegemonic interests in the world. For example, in many countries around the world, the post-9/11 political reporting tended to adapt to the "war on terror discourse/narrative" and its embedded US interests (Nohrstedt & Ottosen 2004).

On relations and reification

In contrast to Leftist media, including "Leftist global journalism" of the kind mentioned here, it is possible to identify a Western and pro-capitalist kind of news discourse, which includes much of Liberal and Conservative thinking. These liberal and conservative media instead tend to portray the world primarily as atomistic, individualized, and fragmented, in which places, events, issues, crises, etc., tend to appear as rather disconnected (Berglez 2004). In other words, they are not that keen on framing and explaining social reality as *one* global totality which is potentially driven and controlled by capitalist interests (Harvey 2007; Phelan 2007). Again, a rather useful Marxist concept is reification (Lukács 1971) and the idea that capitalist societies, due to their widespread fetishistic relation to commodities and commodity exchange, primarily tend to conceive social reality as isolated "things" (events, actions, places, etc.). What reified discourse thus represses is the (globally) relational kind of thinking which instead "emphasizes ...the networks of social relations" (Wayne 2003: 193) and everything's "...interdependence with everything else" (Wayne 2003: 194), including the interdependent relation between the Global North and Global South and the negative consequences for the latter. From a Leftist perspective, besides the fact that media capitalists (Murdock, Berlusconi, and others) own and control hegemonic media in Western countries, the idea is that these media are supporting the market capitalist ideology by their constant production of reified outlooks on society, while global journalism is supposed to challenge this reified rationale of (bourgeois) news journalism.

Economic global journalism (global business news) and ideology

It is possible to argue that global journalism primarily tends to interplay with (global) hegemonic interests in the case of economic information and, more precisely, in the case of (global) financial/business news. Hence, it is possible to observe ideological division, and conflict, between the Leftist-oriented extra-economic global journalism and economic global journalism (global business news). From a Marxist point of view, it would be argued that the business news of Reuters, Bloomberg, Dow Jones and similar services tend to deliver a global news discourse, which is highly reified. At first glance, it might seem as if this kind of news provides us with non-reified information in terms of the emphasis on the *totality* of the global financial system and its complex relations between nations, organizations, and markets. However, the point here is that they constantly cover society and the world in a very abstract and alienating way in terms of a constant flow of figures and stock market results (Kjaer & Slaata 2007). More precisely, in such news, the global economic system and its "mood," fluctuations, and consequences in terms of devastation of national economies, meltdowns, unemployment, and material inequalities tend to appear as natural phenomena beyond human reach and society's ability to control, thereby promoting neoliberalism (a free market beyond the control of states and political organizations) and the elite and upper-middle class who benefit from this ideology (Klein 2008). In other words, it is reified due to its lack of *socially relational discourse*, focusing on, for example, the democratic and ecological consequences of economic globalization.

In conclusion

It is possible to argue that global journalism is not echoing some particular ideological mode of thinking/writing but is rather a basic mode of reporting which might interplay with different ideologies: it might operate as a market capitalism-friendly type of business information as well as a rather Leftist-oriented kind of reporting. However, if global journalism becomes too ideological in one or another direction, it decreases its ability to attract more diverse groups of audiences/users as well as to establish a popular *glopo culture*. It then is dismissed either as propagandistic information for people with genuinely Leftist and anti-market capitalist views or as neoliberal news designed for the capitalist elite and the already privileged. However, somehow, this is the case with all types of journalism. If the production of local information in a particular local paper becomes entirely dominated by a Leftist, Rightist, or Liberal ideology, some news audiences/users will react negatively and turn to other media sources. Therefore, the only thing that could help global journalism to avoid ideological pitfalls is to apply the basic principles of objectivity. But, the art is to do so without losing the (ideological) ability to, when needed, abandon the balance principle by explicitly taking a stand for repressed groups and interests in today's globalizing society in the name of democracy, freedom, and justice (Berglez 2003).

EDUCATIONAL CHALLENGES

To begin with, it is important to point out that journalism programs may look rather different in different countries (see Franklin & Mensing 2011; Löffelholz & Weaver 2008; de Beer & Merrill 2008). However, despite this condition, a common challenge for the world's journalism educators ought to be to overcome the relative absence of global journalism in training. According to Deuze (2008), today's journalism educators often seem to navigate their programs in the transnational or global direction, "... educators everywhere seem to assume that tomorrow's journalist should be able to connect the local to the global...." (Deuze 2008; 270). But is this actually the case? A quick scan of programs offered in European countries, the US, and Asia confirms that international/transnational/global journalism is still offered as a niche competence instead of as a standard element in journalism programs in general. What still tends to be the case in many countries is a strong relationship between journalism education and a national outlook on society. This leaves us with a journalism education

> ...which because of its national bearings is increasingly losing touch with the everyday lived experiences of its intended audiences, who feel either swept away by seemingly uncontrollable global events (terrorism, global warming, worldwide migration, stock market crashes), or hopelessly tied up with narrow-minded and reactionary local affairs. (Deuze 2008: 269)

More precisely, the problem is the intertwined relationship between nation-state institutions (politics, media, education, etc.) and their joint reproduction and naturalization of the nation-state order. For example, a journalism program initiated by the Swedish government and funded by Swedish taxes is somehow supposed to support journalistic practices that primarily focus on the Swedish nation. In a way, this is not particularly unusual, as most of the journalism students will end up in media companies in their home country rather than in transnational media networks and companies. But journalism educators ought to take on the same challenge as the world's media practitioners (journalists and editors), which is to overcome the conception that society is still more or less synonymous with "domestic affairs" and activities that solely take place *within* the national territory, and to instead develop the nation-state-in-the-world-rationale (and the idea of the globalizing society). Training on how to cover the domestic reality (i.e., including the local) needs to become more advanced and complex, globally speaking. However, the idea here is not that, for example, journalism educators in Sweden should repress or even abandon Swedish/domestic affairs but rather that they should, in the context of training, develop the students' ability to also cover them from a post-national point of view (Berglez 2011b).

But what about all the journalism programs that still strive to transcend the national borders? In this context, when it comes to the origin of the students and the trainers, many programs suffer from a national and/or ethnic homogeneity. Here, the risk might be that, even if theory on international communication or global journalism is included in the syllabus, a too "provincial" rationale will keep its grip on the training. Furthermore, simultaneously, my impression is that international journalism programs in Europe and the US which attract students from around the world, including developing countries, do not automatically generate a dynamic "cosmopolitan" training environment as the trainers do not necessarily take maximum advantage of the fact that the participants have different origins. However, there are positive examples as well. When Roland Stanbridge and Stig A. Nohrstedt created the Nordic MA program in Global Journalism at Örebro University in 2004, the original intention was to promote a cosmopolitan view on journalism and to stimulate "transnational journalistic activity" (Grieves 2011: 240; 2012), i.e., to transcend national journalism cultures. In cooperation with colleagues in Tampere and Helsinki, Finland (Kaarle Nordenstreng and Ullamaija Kivikuru), and in Oslo, Norway (Rune Ottosen), the idea was to gather students from all parts of the world. However, despite a global combination of students, the introduction of *global outlooks* could still be a hard challenge. For example, my own (multiannual) teaching experience from this program is that we sometimes dwell on the particular conditions in, and differences between, countries and national journalism cultures instead of concentrating on common global problems and their journalistic challenges. Finally, even if a combination of students from various parts of the world would be the ideal situation, I do not mean that training ethnically and/or nationally homogeneous groups in global journalism is impossible and worthless. Basically, the training should be about integrating the global outlook into regular journalism, and this could be done with a group consisting of only Swedes, Danes, or Turks.

In order to overcome the residual traditions in the field of journalism education, and especially the ones that interplay with the traditional national outlook, educators/trainers could apply the following useful motivational principles suggested by Deuze (2008):

- Paradigm: what (set of) ideas guide journalism education?
- Mission: what is the position of journalism education vis-à-vis the profession and its publics?
- Orientation: on what aspect (or aspects) of journalism is the education based (e.g., the media, genres, or functions of journalism in society)?
- Direction: what are the ideal characteristics of those graduating?
- Contextualization: in what social context is journalism education grounded?
- Education: is journalism education a socializing or an individualizing agent?
- Curriculum: how is the balance between practical and contextual knowledge resolved?
- Method: what is the structural or preferred pedagogy and why?
- Management and organization: how is journalism education organized?

(Deuze 2008: 271)

If they relate to Deuze's concepts, it ought to be an easy task for global journalism trainers to develop and offer such programs (*paradigm*) although the *mission* might collide with the expectations of the media business sector as well as other organizations such as national journalist syndicates which might cultivate a nationally "protectionist" view of the profession. The *orientation* of global journalism in terms of its role in society could build on the same principles as previous generations, that is, to enhance democratic participation in society, to critically investigate power, and so forth. Global journalists are trained in the *context* of a globalizing society, and their *education* needs to engage in the professional mainstreaming of a global journalistic mode of reporting (i.e., its development as a general routine instead of as a niche skill). In order to avoid programs in which global journalism remains a theoretical/ethical ideal or academic buzzword, we must create a *curriculum* and *method* that deal with globalizing society both in theoretical and practical respects and decisively *manage* and *organize* entire education programs in such a direction.

5

Global Journalism and the Digital Web

As was pointed out at the end of chapter 3, despite the existence of a World Wide Web, the Internet is hardly flooded with global outlooks. Like traditional media (press, television, and radio), the digital news flow is suffering from a lack of global news discourse. The global dissemination of *YouTube* videos and other types of social media messages (tweets, etc.) does not count. Such activities might occasionally create global public spheres (Volkmer 1999), but what I have in mind is journalistic coverage on the Web which actively seeks to deliver global outlooks on society. What is paradoxical is that the most global medium ever, the Internet, is not actually very global. It is a well-known fact that, culturally speaking, the Internet is very much a national phenomenon, dominated by domestic news consumption and use of information. Thereby the Web becomes yet another platform for the reproduction of the traditional national outlook on society in which the surrounding world is viewed as "foreign places." Halavais (2000) concluded more than ten years ago, that "...the world wide web conforms to some degree to traditional national borders..." (Halavais 2000: 7), and that is still the case.

To a certain degree, this problem has to do with the way in which the digital technology is applied in actual news reporting. Those news companies which intend to be truly global, must develop new ideas (Heinrich 2011, 2012). I do not claim to have any ultimate answers on this issue, particularly not from a commercial point of view (such as a "business model" for global journalism). But, I would still like to take the opportunity to discuss ways in which global journalism could be digitally presented in the context of web news. News journalism should respond to its identity crisis and "liquid" state (Deuze 2007) by moving in a global direction in which traditional routines, ideals, and values are dynamically combined with the inherent potentials of the digital Web

(Heinrich 2012; cf. Hirst 2011; Berger 2009). In this context, provided that journalists and editors do not simply conform to but also manage to steer available media technology in a desired direction, digital news solutions could really help to establish a post-Westphalian news journalism and break up the traditional reproduction of domestic outlooks on society.

This chapter consists of three sections: first, the potentials as well as pitfalls of Web-driven news journalism will be analyzed in relation to the issue of objectivity and whether the Web could work as a platform for interaction between professional journalism and citizen participation. This will be done in the context of the famous debate between John Dewey and Walter Lippmann on the democratic role of news media in society (see Carey 1992; Berglez 1999; Whipple 2005; Schudson 2008). The dialectics between Lippmann's emphasis on relevant and pertinent news media and Dewey's emphasis on media pluralism is very applicable to today's digital media landscape. Second, by means of poststructuralist theory and the concepts of *hyperlinking* and *hypertextuality*, I will examine the relationship among global processes, the Web, and news journalism. Thanks to the relational (network-oriented) nature of the Internet (Castells 2001), the Web ought to be endowed with unique potential to serve news journalism's representations of complex, global relations (cf. Jameson 1991), which, more precisely, could be done by global hypertexts and hyperlinking. In the final section, I will present and analyze existing as well as potential examples of such news journalism on the Web.

DEWEY, LIPPMANN, AND GLOBAL JOURNALISM ON THE WEB

The Dewey-Lippmann debate on the media, the public, and the democratic role of journalism in society is well known to most media and communication scholars. It all began with Lippmann's seminal theoretical work, *Public Opinion* (1922/1997), which was followed by Dewey's reply in a review of Lippmann's book and developed in texts such as *The Public and Its Problems* (1927/1954). In *Public Opinion*, Lippmann expressed a rather pessimistic and critical view on the expansion of mass media in American society. He viewed the media as disseminators of propaganda and hidden values, an idea which was also developed by the Frankfurt School and Adorno and Horkheimer (1972). Instead of serving and protecting the democratic interests of the majority population, "the public," the media supported the social status quo and the interests of the elite. The central problem, according to Lippmann, was news journalists' inability to analyze and cover the complexity of modern society, which made journalism a target for miscellaneous propagandistic influences and interests. Instead of pertinent and relevant information, citizens were offered stereotypes containing irrational elements, hidden values, and prejudices, which then, in turn, came to influence public opinion and its political reasoning. In Lippmann's view, media would serve the democratic interests of the public by guaranteeing objective and truthful information. Therefore, he was convinced that journalistic practices needed to rely on a scientific rationale and expertise.

Dewey found these ideas interesting and partly convincing, but unlike Lippmann he viewed the rising mass media in a more optimistic manner. To begin with, for Dewey, democracy was not a matter of top-down dissemination of scientific media information to passive recipients but an ongoing process of pluralism and public participation. Ideally, the media should, in the name of democracy, guarantee the existence of a plurality of voices and stimulate civic engagement in which citizens reach their own subjective truth about society. Besides, Dewey did not believe that science is able to deliver the ultimate truth about reality. Instead, he viewed science as one particular voice amongst others, which included poetry, music, literature, politics, religion, and the media. In this sense, Dewey could be seen as an early representative of postmodernist thinking (Lyotard 1979/1997).

How could one then transfer the Dewey-Lippmann debate to today's digital media landscape (cf. Hermida et al. 2011)? To begin with, Lippmann would probably claim that things are worse now than in the early days of modern society. He would criticize the further expansion of "stereotypes" on the Web that emanate from its enormous amateur culture (Keen 2007)—the millions of blogs, tweets, Facebook accounts, etc.,—and the fact that this information is competing with, and sometimes even outcompeting, traditional news media. Lippmann's hypothetical defense of traditional news media in the emerging social media landscape might then probably be accused of elitism. This is very much how *Public Opinion* has been interpreted among its critics in which its purported elitism is viewed as its Achilles' heel (for another interpretation of this, see Schudson 2008). However, Lippmann would most likely defend his view by emphasizing that today's online communication environment demonstrates citizens' urgent need for qualitative and reliable information. In an increasingly complex world of global relations, run by global and national elites and powerful companies, professional news media institutions, guided by a scientific rationale in the name of journalistic objectivity are required to improve the democratic situation for the non-elite and thus the majority population. What is needed in this new technological environment is an *enhanced* professional news journalism which manages to rigorously check, filter, and organize the vast mass of information in society that is flourishing on the Web and elsewhere.

It seems rather obvious that Dewey would embrace and defend contemporary citizen journalism (Allan & Thorsen 2009) and the explosion of social media activities. The development of social media harmonizes with Dewey's idea that the media should serve as a dynamic space for public participation, characterized by ongoing debates on what is right and wrong, true or false, and so forth. Due to its generation of online voices/sources and digital participations, which might even help to overthrow repressive regimes such as happened in the case of the Arab Spring in 2011, it is possible to assume that Dewey would look favorably upon the Internet and its digital technology.

The global outlook as representation and pluralism

Lippmann and Dewey guide us in different directions. But by selecting important insights from both of them, I intend to combine their contrasting standpoints into one idea as to how global outlooks ought to develop on the Web.

I will begin with Lippmann. When it comes to scientific influences in news journalism, Lippmann has an important point to make. However, like many others I find his position in *Public Opinion* too extreme. For example, I do not believe that the epistemological foundation of global journalism, i.e., the global outlook, either could or should be entirely under the influence of scientific logic or expertise. Journalism is endowed with its own rationale which only partly coincides with scientific views, or more precisely that of the social sciences. For example, both journalists and researchers use the interview method or present theories/hypotheses on how to interpret events, but their practices are in many respects different because the social sciences tend to study social reality in a more rigorous and systematic way than journalism does. At the same time, it is hard to ignore the fact that the concept of global journalism is partly based on social scientific reasoning. I argue throughout this book that the social scientific conclusion that globalization is an ever more important condition (delivered by theorists such as Giddens, Beck, and Castells) should be exported to the field of news journalism. Such an epistemological development of professional journalism would keep news media updated (and thus more democratic and relevant) as society and the entire world develop. Therefore, to some extent, I do believe in Lippmann's imagined standpoint that professional news journalism needs to improve its ability to act as an authoritative voice in the landscape of Web 2.0. Its democratic legitimacy among the public should thus derive from its capability to, as the social sciences do, *represent* the (global) complexity of social reality. Perhaps, our joint statement would be that, in a global world, news journalism needs to regain the initiative and stand out in the digital crowd. It needs to update its basic routines, develop its digital practices, and become a provider of the advanced and professional global outlooks on the Web that citizen journalism and social media in most cases do not provide us with.

However, the Deweyan perspective helps us to understand that in today's digital media landscape, social media and citizen journalism cannot be neglected. Despite the fact that he argued that democracy should primarily be practiced in small-scale societies and communities, Dewey would probably view the production of global outlooks as an important, ongoing cosmopolitan *conversation* on the Internet between citizens and various interest groups from different parts of the world. Contemporary digital media researchers such as Bardoel & Deuze (2001), Deuze (2007), Usher (2010), Hermida (2010) and Heinrich (2011, 2012) argue for the importance of *network journalism*, which, in my view, makes them representatives of *neo-Deweyan* thinking (see Hermida et al. 2011). They all stress that the Web 2.0 revolution and the expansion of UGC, crowd sourcing, the blogosphere, etc., should be seen as givens of the general news flow. Thereby, they pass on Dewey's original idea that media and their technology should primarily stimulate public participation and diversity. In the case of global journalism, professional news journalism should increasingly interact with social media and citizen journalism. They should jointly contribute to a dynamic and pluralist news flow in which traditional methods and routines are combined with the inclusion of a "cosmopolitan" variety of sources/voices made available by means of the Web (Henderson 2009). When defining the global outlook, Heinrich states, "I would add to this definition that a 'global outlook' furthermore takes into account the plurality of voices streaming in from a variety of emerging information channels" (Heinrich 2012: 4). According to Heinrich, traditional news media still tend to neglect the potential of the global Web as a provider of plurality (cf. Livingston & Asmolov 2010). This conclusion is supported by media research which demonstrates that compared to their print editions, traditional news companies' online editions do not generate a higher level of plurality in terms of various perspectives and sources (Gerhards & Schäfer 2010).

The understanding of global outlooks on the Web in relation to the Dewey-Lippmann debate should be summarized by means of the distinction between representation and pluralism, in which Lippmann would be associated with the representation perspective, while Dewey should be associated with pluralism:

> REPRESENTATION: How could professional news journalism on the Web develop qualitative and advanced ways of covering the global condition and its complex relations?
>
> PLURALISM: How could news on the Web include a (global) plurality of voices/sources by means of increasing interactivity between professional news journalism and citizen journalism/social media?

It is clear that they are both relevant, but how should we conceive their relationship? Here, I would like to stress that, in the coverage of an event, a "mosaic" of plural voices from all possible corners of the world will not by itself demonstrate global relations to the news audiences/users. A plurality of voices/sources from all continents does not necessarily generate news discourse which shows more exactly *how* these continents are interconnected. Media coverage might include verbal comments from Russia, Brazil and South Africa but might still end up as the traditional foreign outlook with reports about separate national experiences and conditions which are never interlinked as a global story. Thus, in my view, in the development of global outlooks on the Web, pluralism, i.e., the voices/sources of citizen journalism/social media, needs to be *integrated* in the overall journalistic task of representing global complexities and relations.

GLOBALIZATION, POSTSTRUCTURALISM, AND GLOBAL WEB JOURNALISM

Digital news journalism's potential to represent (i.e., not only to cover but also to narrate) the globalizing society requires a few comments on the *relationship of globalization and the Web*. In this context, poststructuralist theory is useful as it is applicable to both. The poststructuralist theoretical point of departure when approaching globalization as well as the Web is the idea of viewing social reality in terms of a system and/or structure constituted by *complex relations*.

The theory of poststructuralism is primarily associated with certain French philosophers and their post-Marxist (Poster 1989) exploration of society. Their main argument is that society is constituted of processes of differentiation. The theoretical precursor is structuralism, especially the contributions from the linguist Ferdinand de Saussure, in which language plays a central role. At the beginning of the previous century, de Saussure (1974) developed the idea that language is a system regulated by the relationship of the signifier and the signified. What characterizes both structuralist and poststructuralist thinking is the emphasis on differentiation as *relations* between elements which mutually constitute each other. For example, the existence of A presupposes the existence of B, while the present presupposes the absent (Derrida 1978). Every text, as an outcome of meaning-making, is related to, and therefore also constituted by, other texts (intertextual relations) in an ongoing production of structures or systems, networks, or webs. Even the entire society is seen as a "text" based on the constant production of differences and relations among peoples, institutions, places, ideas, production, and so forth. However, what distinguishes structuralism from poststructuralism is the latter's explicit engagement in the idea that social reality is non-fixed and contingent and thus not predetermined by history or some metaphysical principle, be it class struggle, God, the unconscious, or truth (Derrida 1978; Foucault 1984; Lyotard 1979/1997; Laclau & Mouffe 1985).

First, let us look at the poststructuralist understanding of globalization. A key aspect of globalization is relations, be they material, economic, political, technological, or cultural. The post-Marxist thinker, Fredric Jameson (1991; Danius & Jonsson 1993), who is inspired by poststructuralism, tends to see the global condition as a complex "text," or more precisely as complex relations among "texts" which are material, economic, political, technological, cultural, and so forth. Globalization as a textual system has no essential center and is constantly transforming in terms of ongoing dynamic relations between peoples, places, processes, and actions worldwide, in which the late capitalist economy is supposed to be the driving force.[1]

And then there is the poststructuralist understanding of the Web. Naturally, poststructuralist theory could be applied to all kinds of text production, from poetry and literature to television and beyond (Bolter & Grusin 2000), focusing on, for example, the relation between historical and contemporary texts and/or how present/contemporary texts are based on absent/historical texts. However, in the particular case of the Web, "textual relations" appear and operate in a very obvious way, as what defines the Web is basically links between texts/websites and the relations they generate in terms of a networked information and communication system that is constantly transforming and growing (Castells 2001). As the Internet is nothing but an ongoing structure of interconnected texts, it is possible to claim that the Web certainly embodies the basic theoretical principles of poststructuralist theory.

Sometimes, globalization and the Web become one, which then more precisely explains why poststructuralist theory is applicable to both of them. When global relations converge with Web relations (i.e., links) and, vice versa, the Web contributes to a global media culture. Here, we could imagine a communicative process on the Web such as, for example, a YouTube video with political content which becomes globally known and viewed in various parts of the world, such as KONY 2012, a film produced by Missing Children that focuses on the crimes of the guerilla leader Joseph Kony in Central Africa and which so far has generated 91 million hits (Weman 2012).[2]

However, the question is how the practice of global journalism might improve its ability to *represent* the global condition by means of the global Web. In this respect, two postructurally oriented concepts could further assist global journalism's development on the Web—hypertextuality and hyperlinking.

Hypertextuality and hyperlinking

I would like to maintain the idea that, basically speaking, global journalism primarily presupposes the willingness to interconnect seemingly disconnected phenomena across continents. And in order to achieve this, you do not necessarily need the latest media technologies and platforms, not even the Web. At the same time, one can certainly argue that the Web is rather suitable for global journalism. Here, some would stress that global journalism and the Web are perfect matches given the Internet's ability to dynamically bring about the convergence of old and new media (Jenkins 2006). The outcome of convergence, multimodal communication (Vobič 2011), is assumed to have positive consequences for news media's ability to capture global complexity:

> Traditional news media are commercial news organizations that have historically focused on the daily delivery of information concerning a geographic (e.g., local, state, national, international) area in either a textual, audio or visual format offline. In the online realm, audio, video and text can be intertwined to more efficiently create layers that sometimes promote a deeper level of understanding (Carpenter 2010: 1065).

However, in my view, what makes the Web perfectly suitable for global journalism is the Web's ability to interconnect separate pieces of information in terms of web links.[3] More precisely, the *hypertextual* nature of the Web can represent fundamentally "relational" and interdependent phenomena such as the globalizing society. According to Steensen (2011), the "hypertext is generally understood as a computer-based non-linear group of texts (i.e., written text, image, etc.) that are linked together with hyperlinks" (2011: 313; see also Nelson 1982; Bolter & Grusin 2000: 161; Oblak 2005; Buckle 2011: 116–119). One usually distinguishes between internal and external hyperlinking: "Texts, interconnected through links—hyperlinks—can refer internally (to other texts within the text's domain) or externally (to texts located elsewhere on the Internet)" (Deuze 2001: 5). Hyperlinking paves the way for the reporting of more information than in, for example, a newspaper or television news. As link after link could be added to a chain of texts, there is actually no limit. As a result, to some extent, online news has generated new ways of organizing and presenting news, such as in terms of a chain of connected information/links. This chain is continually updated and fed with new links, offering news stories in a state of constant motion and "liquidity" (Karlsson & Strömbäck 2010).

However, in research on computer-mediated communication and in the debate on the development of digital news and journalism on the Web, these two concepts are often associated with great promises which have never been fulfilled (Oblak 2005; Steensen 2011). For different reasons, news media companies tend to avoid linking to information outside their own archives and domains. When it comes to the further development of hypertextual news production, traditional news providers have too often simply transferred old modes of communication to the Web "...continuing a long history of resisting innovation and new techniques" (Barnhurst 2012: 1; see also Barnhurst 2010). Thus, the potentials of hyperlinking have not yet been entirely explored, at least not in the global sense.

In this context, some tend to merely associate the global potential of hypertexts with their assumed ability to generate greater pluralism (diversity) in media content (Carpenter 2010), in which the increasing interactivity of professional journalism and citizen journalism/social media is highlighted. However, in line with the idea of representation and pluralism discussed above, I suggest that the role of citizen journalism/social media needs to be integrated in a theory where the point of departure is how hypertextuality/hyperlinking could help professional news journalism to refresh its *coverage* of the globalizing society in a more fundamental sense.

More precisely, what one should pay attention to is how:

A. the relations of the globalizing society, and;
B. the relations of the Web (hyperlinks),

could interplay in

C. the reporting practice and the production of news content (for example, when demonstrating the relationship of the local and global in the coverage of an event).

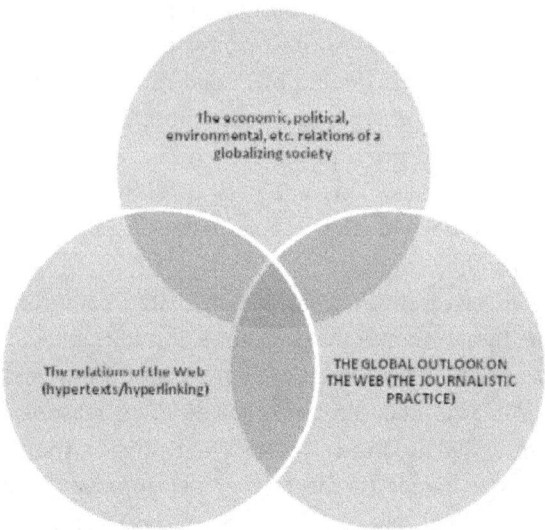

Figure 5.1. Global Journalism on the Web

By decisively combining the global outlook with hypertextual practices (hyperlinking) in the production, editing, and presentation of news, the complex relations of the globalizing society could emerge in dynamic ways. This cognitive and discursive competence is still missing in news journalism. It is true that the entire Internet is flooded with hypertextual activities and information products. But still, who should take the responsibility for developing a hypertextual coverage that helps us to more clearly experience the global condition by means of the Web and for transforming this into everyday news discourse in support of glopo culture if not professional news journalists?

Global Journalism and the Digital Web

Global hyperlinking and hypertexts

It is important to consider the hyper practices of online communication, not as some Web technique that merely extends or complements a news story with more information but as a fundamental mode of communicating social reality and, therefore, as a "narrative style" (cf. Buckle 2011). In this context, in concrete reporting of a global crisis or issue, the very acts of hyperlinking should also capture a global relation of some kind (technological, economic, political, social, ecological, cultural, etc.)

GLOBAL HYPERLINKS  GLOBAL RELATIONS

Instead of solely producing a global outlook in the traditional sense, for example in terms of oral narration or voiceover in a news story for television and/or as a written text (the news article), the actual interdependent relationship of Asia, Africa and Europe concerning, for example, the spread of an epidemic disease, could be journalistically represented by the very organization and arrangement of hyperlinked Web links. Or, the coverage of how Swedish water consumption is affecting the water situation in other parts of the world, should be presented as hyperlinks to

(i) news information on water consumption in Sweden;
(ii) news information on how Swedish water consumption is affecting the water situation in Moscow, Ljubljana, and Cairo, and;
(iii) news information on the water situation in affected countries worldwide.

Thus, the hyperlinks should achieve an elucidative mirroring of the global relations. Naturally, this kind of hyperlinking does occasionally occur in mainstream Web news, for example, in various global crisis reporting in which the main news Web pages might be hyperlinked to Web pages which present political reactions and social consequences in various countries and parts of the world. However, we should imagine this as far more sophisticated versions of what is actually the case today—as advanced *global hypertexts* and *global hyperlinking* in the form of discursive weaves of intercontinental relations.

Here, a possible objection might be that when using external links, there could be firewall restrictions, multilingual barriers, and lack of juridical rights to access the desired Web information. However, to a great extent, hyperlinking could also be based on *internal* Web links and material provided by the media producers themselves. In accordance with previous reasoning on the relationship of pluralism and representation, hyperlinking should not simply be synonymous with delivering a global mixture of sources (pluralism) from different websites but an overall mode of "narrating" the global outlook (representation). Thus, in the reporting of a hypertextual global "universe," except for relevant knowledge about the reported issue, perhaps what is mainly required is innovative hypertextual thinking by editors and journalists, not a vast number of external links.

In order to clarify how this kind of Web journalism could be developed in various ways, I will return to the three cognitive categories central to global journalism, namely, space, power, and identity (see chapter 2).

Space

When we are online, to what extent do we sense the Web as a global kind of space, in which the entire world is gathered or present? It is well known that in the context of everyday website clicking, that is, when jumping from website to website, our movements might be dominated by behaviors and routines which rather obscure the global dimension of the Web. This could be the consequence of solely domestic (national) consumption of websites (Halavais 2000) and social media or of the dominance of US/Western Web information. Our movements and orientation on the Web might simply not be driven by the desire to capture the global world or the like, but by other information and communication needs.

Naturally, we should not forget about the "cosmopolitan" nomadic subjects whose net activities (playing computer and video games, using social media, etc.) generate connections and input from all corners of the world. However, not even in these cases, does a *global space* necessarily appear, as, despite the Web's establishment of transnational connections, the "cosmopolitan" subject's virtual jumping from one place/website to another might remind us of, not a "global walk" from one continent to another but a pinball ball's propulsion from node to node which might seem rather *spaceless*. Thus, the point is that the virtual jump from continent to continent on the Web does not guarantee the sense of a global house with a common roof, or a "village" (McLuhan 2001). On the contrary, it might rather repress the experience of global space as a common universe endowed with interdependent relations and shared responsibility.

An important reason for this is the Web's abolishment of the material qualities that "real" global space possesses—places, territories, borders, routes, terrains, etc. When it comes to new media and media technology, their capacity to compress and minimize time-space distance is always highlighted (Carey 1992; Falkheimer & Jansson 2006). This is then what makes it possible for Internet users to transport themselves on the Web from one continent to another with extreme speed. But, at the same time, as a consequence, when "travelling through space," the sense of travelling disappears. Unhampered and timeless movement in space blurs the actual sense of place (Meyrowitz 1985) and the human experience of borders, i.e., the concrete characteristics of the route which stretches from A to B, for example, the shifting landscape when travelling from Sweden to Uganda.

However, this (de-spatial) development might pave the way for the re-"materialization" of space on the Web in terms of advanced representations of the global universe as intertwined "roads" or connections between different places. News journalism could deliver the relational contours of global space by exploring the communicative advantages of the Web. What I am getting at is something which would go beyond the usual graphic maps of the globe (see the nuclear weapon article in chapter 2). By means of hypertextual news coverage it is possible to organize the relation between the (news) Web pages as global transportation, which, in turn, is supposed to simulate human movement between places in global space.

MOVEMENT BETWEEN WEB SITES  MOVEMENT IN GLOBAL SPACE

Basically, what makes this possible is a kind of storytelling which narrates how various places are connected (economically, environmentally, and so forth). Thus, a well-defined (global) pathway could be journalistically directed and designed in which the news audiences/users are actively *escorted* from place to place, where they intermingle with various transnational experiences, ideas, forecasts, explanations. In this way, the virtual transportation from Stockholm to the rural outskirts of Sao Paulo and Perth in a news story about the production and use of ethanol fuel is ideally *experienced* as a global walk.

Power

Power relations tend to interconnect various places around the globe, especially those of the economic and political kind, involving stakeholders such as governments, multinational enterprises, organizations, and particular individuals. The Web ought to become important when it comes to news journalism's making global power relations more visible and graspable. By means of the Web it becomes possible to better illustrate complex causal relations and trace their actual or assumed consequences at the intercontinental and even global level. The potential of the Web is not only to be found in its ability to present power relations by means of ever more advanced graphics and/or in terms of numerous non-professional interpretations and eye-witnessing through social media. Here, what is intended is a hypertextual news journalism which increasingly allows the news audiences/users to "jump" between various presented global causes, and/or offers a digital pathway illustrating the entire "causes to effects" process. The point would be to, in the very structuring and presentation of the news, create a cognitive and discursive analogy to the actual global power relations:

THE CHAIN OF CAUSAL POWER RELATIONS  A CHAIN OF HYPERLINKS

This might be interwoven with the following topics, which in one way of another touch upon power relations—how the water consumption and policies in one particular country affect the water situation in other countries; the portrayal of the transnational consequences of a particular country's CO_2 emissions in various respects; the ways in which consumer patterns and behavior in one part of the world affect social well-being in another part of the world; the decision processes behind a business relocation from one part of the world to another; the motifs and actions involved in the outsourcing of certain services to distant countries, or the explanation of a global power's particular action (the EU, the US, OECD, etc.) and its assumed or actual consequences in various countries:

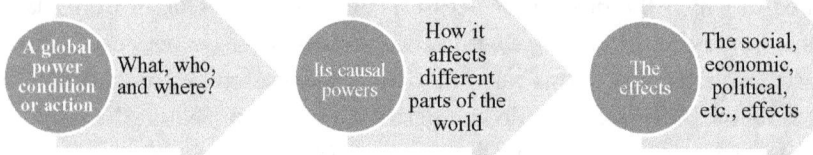

Figure 5.2: The Hypertextual Organization of Global Causes

A hypertextual rationale could also help to achieve more vivid presentations of massive and complex material such as, for example, the kind of documents WikiLeaks usually provides its global audience with, that is, information on "government and corporate misconduct" (cf. Handley & Ismail 2012).

Furthermore, the complex power relations presented in the poststructuralist theory of Foucault and his followers (Hardt & Negri 2000, and others) could be covered in hypertextual fashion on how global macro-power (of governments, multinational companies, the OECD, etc.) is constituted at the micro-level of society (in our everyday routines and behavior, consumption, language use, through our bodies, etc.). What also ought to become mainstream Web news in the near future are hypertextually structured stories about the Web itself. For example, news coverage in which the audiences/users are offered simulated "underground" tours on the Internet, focusing on encryption and the consequences of our daily Web clicking and the digital footprints we tend to make; on how and where particular footprints are stored, packaged, and exploited by various (macro-power) agents in an ever more complex global network environment.

Identity

Global crises and issues usually involve populations in different parts of the world. Therefore, as part of reporting the global outlook, news media must seek to develop their ability to include voices from the entire globe. More precisely, this is a matter of news media's handling of identity, i.e., the potential end result of an identification process among individuals and/or groups, which might be based on ethnicity, ideology, religion, culture, politics, class, gender or sexual orientation (Olausson 2009a). As has already been mentioned, when it comes to the digital Web, increasing interactivity between traditional news journalism and social media might definitely pave the way for the inclusion of plural identities in the news media and thus a dynamic combination of voices from different parts of the world (cf. Heinrich 2011, 2012).

The issue which arises here is how news journalism on the Web could find even more advanced ways of using the enormous flow of global sources and move beyond the recent trend of treating the world's population mainly as a source of eyewitness comments and digital amateur material (photos, videos), emanating from tweets or mobile phones. How could social media material contribute even more to professional news reporting? In my view, global voices from social media have more depth in the news if they are there in order to, for example, portray identity processes that a global crisis event or a global power issue might trigger or in order to deepen the coverage of a local event (How is this issue or problem handled among other people and groups in other parts of the world?). Assume there is a terror attack in the country of A: how do groups of people react to this event in different parts of the world, including our own region, and how are they affected by it at the macro- and micro-levels of life? This kind of approach has been present in domestic news media in extreme crises, such as in the coverage of 9/11 (Berglez 2006) and the tsunami catastrophe in 2004 (Riegert et al. 2010; Robertson 2010), but by means of the Web, the inclusion of the world's comments on all kinds of globally salient matters could become naturalized, i.e., a taken-for-granted element in everyday news.

Consequently, the basic method and routine should be to discursively embroider the covered event with continuous comments from laymen as well as experts from different parts of the world, in which the practice of hyperlinking ought to play an important role. In this context, one could also imagine the further development of "global chats" which might take place in parallel with the coverage of an event: consequently there would be cross-continental discussions among, and in front of, the news audiences/users. The news coverage could offer their audiences/users digital (hyperlinked) "walks" between the very coverage of the event and one or several public spheres, in which "the global world" could gather in order to comment and exchange ideas on the latest developments. Here, we need to imagine more advanced examples than the "cross-continental conversation" between two households, one in Sweden and the other in the Maldives on the climate issue (see chapter 2). Through cooperation between media houses in different parts of the world as well as among media houses and social media by ever more advanced ways of including UGC in news reporting among news editors, global reactions and comments could become much more of a mainstream routine among the world's news producers. Imagine, for example, how the reporting of a domestic event in a (small) local Web newspaper could be complemented with input from people in other countries who have similar experiences. At the very least, this could pave the way for a (global) journalism which might establish discursive bridges (Olausson 2005) between common identities and groups around the world and/or dynamic conversations between different identity positions. Naturally, this already takes place in numerous social media, chat rooms, and forums on the Internet, but when such activities are transferred to professional Web news journalism, they become less marginal and elite oriented and could therefore play a more important role in society (remember glopo culture). More precisely, they could more easily contribute to the

Global Journalism and the Digital Web

mainstream political debate and perhaps influence political decisions at the domestic as well as global level. If the world of politics is unable to establish global democratic public spheres beyond the UN (Fraser 2007), then the news media in numerous countries might achieve this in the context of everyday reporting.

Three ways of identifying global journalism on the Web

Now, we should move from the normative discussion on the need for a more advanced kind of global journalism on the Web to the question of how to empirically identify existing examples of such news reporting. Table 5.1 thus summarizes the way in which space, power, and identity could be used as a point of departure for analyzing the presence/absence of (hypertextual) global journalism on the Web:

Table 5.1. Global Journalism on the Web from Three Perspectives

Category	Digital Web potentials
SPACE	To what extent is hyperlinking practiced in order to interconnect places worldwide, thereby representing social reality as a shared global space?
POWER	To what extent is hyperlinking practiced in order to capture the "cause and effect" pathways of power processes in a global context?
IDENTITY	To what extent is hyperlinking practiced in order to include the world's various political, ethnical, or cultural voices in the global journalistic coverage?

GLOBALIZING NEWS DISCOURSE ON THE WEB

Below, I have sought to illustrate global journalism on the Web "in full." Each and every box represents a Web page. The boxes are hyperlinked and one is supposed to jump in between them. Furthermore, all boxes are potentially hyperlinked to other (external) links. The news audiences/users are supposed to transport themselves between the boxes in a space of transnational information and communication. Altogether, the available websites and links represent a global outlook on the covered event, be it a terrorist attack with transnational consequences or the trafficking problem in various parts of the world:

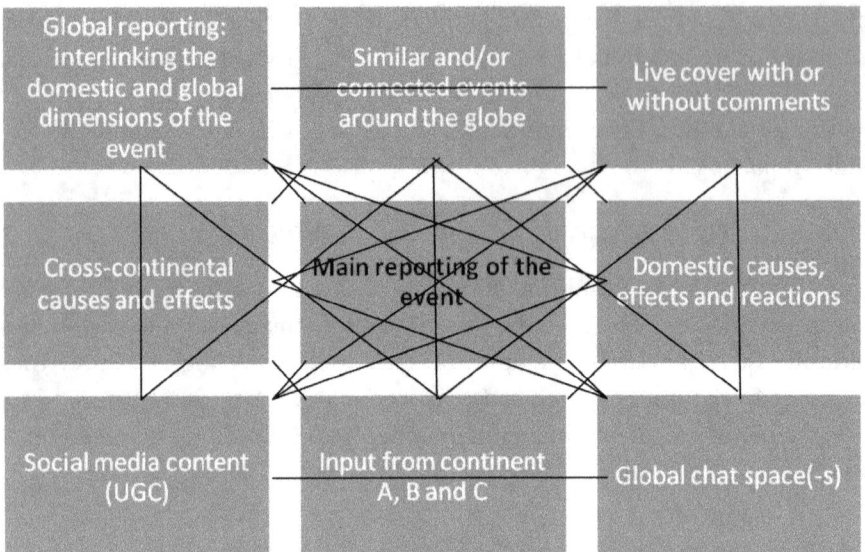

Figure 5.3 Globalizing News Discourse on the Web

The rather traditional gulf between the domestic ("Domestic causes, effects and reactions") and the foreign world (present in most other boxes) could be avoided by means of discursive *integration*. Certain information in each and every box needs to be presented in the other boxes as well. More precisely, the particular reporting on domestic causes, effects and reactions should discursively integrate input from other countries, analysis of cross-continental causes and effects, and verbal reactions from the global chat space, and so forth. Thus, ideally, what drives the news audience/users to orient themselves in this digital landscape is extra material on matters which have already been presented in some other box. While moving from box to box, the audiences/users not only learn about but also get a concrete sense of the interconnections between different parts of the world.

Naturally, quality in news journalism primarily presupposes qualified reporters and editors and sufficient economic resources to send correspondents into the field and for research and fact-checking. However, when it comes to the further development of global journalism on the Web one should not underestimate the role of design. According to the award-winning news Web designer Jacek Utko (2009), when building a Web platform for online news one needs to ask the following question: "What is the purpose of this object and building this product?" (p. 1). Consequently, global journalism on the Web presupposes the construction of a particular Web architecture which allows for advanced demonstrations of global relations in everyday news reporting. If global journalism becomes squeezed into the standard way of designing news webs, the production and presentation of news are likely to collapse into the traditional national outlook on society.

Epilogue

The purpose of this book has been to contribute to the theoretical development of the idea of global journalism as well as to analyze its present practice in the news. In this epilogue using a short question-and-answer format, my central points and arguments will be repeated and/or clarified.

Why did you write so much about domestic news journalism (local reporting as well as national media) in this book? Was not this book supposed to be about GLOBAL journalism? My intention was to underline the idea that global journalism has no natural connection to global news media (i.e., transnational media companies and information that reach global audiences/users) and that they definitively are not synonymous (very often, this is exactly how global journalism is interpreted). When it comes to mainstream news, the future of global journalism is primarily to be found in your local news Web or in national broadcast media. It is not the opposite of local journalism or the national news but a natural continuation of these traditional forms of covering social reality. Consequently, I do not imagine the potential expansion of global journalism in terms of a *radical* paradigm shift in the history of modern news, as the important ingredient, the global outlook, is rather supposed to evolve within the "old" media paradigm (in "normal" local reporting and national news and so forth). But still, it would indicate a very important shift in the history of news with far-reaching consequences. We should conceive it as a global discursive news movement which develops from "below," i.e., not in the editorial milieus of Al Jazeera and BBC World but in hundreds of thousands of local and national news media. At the end of the day, it is the local and national regions worldwide which really need global outlooks in order to cope with an ever more integrated globe.

The kind of news journalism which I have in mind.... is it really not too expensive for most media companies? Global journalism is not more or less expensive than other forms of reporting. The global outlook does not primarily presuppose expensive airline tickets and foreign offices, an expensive media technical apparatus, or an impressively large multimedia news desk but rather a new mode of *interpreting* social reality in regular news reporting. Besides the traditional methods and routines such as interviews, rigorous fact-checking, double-checking of sources, etc., it could also include various transnational journalistic methods, such as the expansion of international journalistic networks for the identification of contextual information and sources and new global hyperlinking routines on the Web for the presentation of globalizing news. I dare to claim that the work routines of global journalism are not more costly than journalistic work routines in general. However, before news journalists manage to integrate the global outlook in the regular "speedy tempo" of media logic, high costs will probably be incurred in terms of extra time for research and background material as well as for the global journalistic "packaging" of stories.

But wouldn't most journalists find it too complex to rapidly and repeatedly include global outlooks in their reporting? Instead of viewing it as an everyday competence, both media/journalism researchers and practicing journalists tend to associate global journalism with advanced methods which only a few professionals know how to manage. However, this critical question and the way it is posed ("Wouldn't most journalists find it too complex...?") tend to obscure the fact that today's established practices once were considered complex "innovations" as well. Consequently, too often it is assumed that today's routines were natural routines from the very beginning. Furthermore, the taken-for-granted domestic outlook in contemporary news journalism, especially the national outlook, is the end result of numerous historical conflicts on how to organize society as well as political and cultural forces in the name of nationalism. At least, this is what Anderson (1991) and others' research on the birth, development, and establishment of the nation-state and the role of media tends to indicate. In other words, the routines required for a regular implementation of the global outlook could become "naturalized" and also become taken for granted provided that they are continually practiced in the field and in editorial milieus as well as taught in journalism schools. Probably, the sum of these actions will generate ever more refined ways of integrating the global reality in the everyday news.

Why this constant emphasis on climate reporting and business news? Because these modes of reporting can be seen as the modern product (business news) and "perfect" example (climate reporting) of global journalism. I argue that the development of global journalism in mainstream news media should be a case of extending the (basic) global relational rationale of business journalism to all other news areas and topics. When it comes to climate change, this global crisis is of such a magnitude and existential relevance that it ought to have the power to shape the future of news journalism as such. Not only should the climate issue be "adjusted" to existing media logic (in which complex climate science is transformed into news that is comprehensible to the public), but media logic should "adjust" to the logic of the crisis in terms of delivering a discursive counterpart to the boundless and relational nature of climate change.

But why do not Twitter and other social media serve as the ultimate kind of global journalism (as their scope, networking rationale, and communication are potentially much more global than most traditional news media)? Social media might be perfect tools for supporting the generation of global outlooks. For example, they could be very helpful in establishing a network of multinational sources, which could be used in news reporting. But, social media flows, containing separate pieces of information from different parts of the world, could hardly themselves establish the kind of relational discourse that is required in order to establish a global outlook. You still need an "author" who, in the form of a story, narrates how the actual event (the terror attack, the environmental crisis, or the business event) involves cross-continental relations. And this is why the "collective intelligence" of Google could not easily replace global journalism. Google Search provides us with a transnational and culturally diverse smorgasbord of information about and images (Google Earth) of the globe, but these media technologies do not provide us with discursive demonstrations of global interconnectivities.

Don't you harp a little too much on the important role of global journalism for the entire future of news journalism? In addition to your ideas on advanced hyperlinking practices on the Web, can you explain more precisely how this future kind of journalism should be imagined, let's say 50 years from now? What would the "science fiction" version of global journalism look like? Roughly speaking, perhaps this is the way in which global journalism will be described in retrospect:

Actually, today's established (global) journalism is a relatively young mode of reporting. The late 1990s and the first decades of this century were a time of great transformation. When the digital Web turned into a universal tool, the already porous ground on which professional journalism was standing finally cracked. Societies overflowed with news, or more precisely with news-like information which outcompeted traditional news. Potentially, everybody was able to make "news," and everyone could turn into news. So, what was the "traditional" journalist supposed to do? Do the same thing as hundreds of millions of others but slightly better? Perhaps so, but who would want to pay for it? The answer is: very few. At this time, social media experts preached the end of journalism while media scholars wrote books with alarmist titles such as *Journalism: What Is It Good for (Who Needs It)?* or *Journalism Is Dead*. But, instead, the bleak situation caused dialectical movement and the identification of new communicative challenges. The global crises and issues before and after the millennium shift (especially the democratic and political explosion of the Web, the nuclear issue, the dramatic melting of the North Pole, and the water crisis) clarified the contours of the globalizing society and nations became deeply connected and interdependent. A new (global) reality had arrived, but who was supposed to take care of the discursive side of it: the everyday narration of events? Not the "man in the street" who was still occupied with producing the old, "pre-global" information by means of his/her mobile phone…. Thus, there was a need for skilled people who could quickly narrate but also visualize and explain all the complex but still newsworthy causal relations that humans were capable of creating in an ever more integrated world and which were increasingly embedded in all kinds of domestic events. Altered methods of covering and narrating social reality were increasingly requested, which was a suitable task for a new generation of communicative professionals, i.e., *journalists* with important assistance from other types of media practitioners and practices. In this way, the perfect job opportunity finally popped up for the "old" (unemployed) reporter who gradually reclaimed his/her democratic and "enlightening" role in a dramatically shifting media landscape.

The typical kind of global journalistic coverage? Here is what one journalist says:

> I would like to mention a story I did the other day about the emergent energy crisis and its effects on European households. Quickly I arranged a transnational chat with people in ten different countries about their various fears and in some cases rather drastic experiences. It was combined with our earth-transcendence (Web) technology, in which they were sent on a virtual journey to the actual natural gas sources, through the actual Nord Stream pipe line, all the way to Western Siberia. The point is that my number one rule as news journalist is that the cross-continental relations which surround the re-

ported event, be it a social, environmental, economic or cultural relation, need to be, not only clearly explained, but also perceived among the news audiences/users. The "victim" of some distant power action should experience the (distant) source of his/her problem in the very reporting. The seven-minute coverage was immediately translated into 44 languages, and as my newspaper collaborates with numerous newspapers in various countries, it reached out to 200 million (potential) readers/users. I think that this is when journalism is at its best; as an informative and analytical service that connects peoples, places and actions across the world!

Notes

Chapter 1. Global Journalism: An Introduction

1. It seems evident that global journalism research is a diverse field which gathers scholars who are internationally oriented and who want to act outside the "national box" by actively questioning national, cultural, and disciplinary boundaries as is the case with Löffelholz's & Weaver's book (2008: 3-4). I sympathize with this approach, but this eagerness to transcend all kinds of distinctions and borders might also partly explain the generic characteristics of the global journalism concept. Perhaps for too long we have used this concept as a general logo for our "internationalist" or cosmopolitan ideals as journalism researchers rather than for empirical analyses of the truly global in journalistic practice. A sign of this is the global journalism concept's tendency to represent all that is not domestic. In other words, in one way or another, the global tends to represent a research interest in *other* nations or continents. Besides, some journalism studies might thus have better forgone the "global" prefix, as they deal with international aspects of media and journalism among nation-states. Somewhat paradoxically, the imprecise meaning of the concept sometimes even paves the way for a traditional national outlook on journalism (see Berglez 2008) or "methodological nationalism" as Beck (2006: 24) coins it. For example, in de Beer & Merrill (2008) and Löffelholz & Weaver's (2008) anthologies, some contributions tend to fall back into traditional comparisons (cf. Wasserman 2010: 4-5) of national journalism systems or cultures. As Cottle (2011) emphasizes: "Too often the title of 'global journalism' simply serves as an encompassing/descriptive term or as a reference for comparative discussion of different national media systems and the discerned states of national journalism, losing analytical purchase and use value in the process (Cottle 2011: 20). Hence, it is reasonable to suggest that the concept simply cannot encompass everything that has to do with journalism in various countries. In order to make it more efficient for empirical analyses as well as training, we need to distinguish what global journalism is from what it is not.

2. This kind of critique also derives from those who hesitate as to the scientific relevance of globalization theory (see Rosenberg 2000) for understanding or explaining contemporary journalism. As Sparks puts it: "Whatever has been going on in the world for the last quarter of a century, this is not the way to theorize it" (2005: 23). In other words, as today's news content is dominated by local and national outlooks, it is often assumed to be a waste of time to focus on global journalism, empirically speaking. A similar kind of skepticism derives from the kind of post-globalization literature in media studies that tends to downplay the importance of

globalization and instead argue for the continuing importance of the nation-state (Calhoun 2007; Roosvall & Salovaara-Moring 2010).

3. In order to avoid misunderstandings, I do embrace the idea of a global journalism as a critical force that seeks to make the world a better place to live in (Wasserman 2010, 2011a) in terms of counteracting neoliberalism, racism, or war discourse (see chapter 4). Furthermore, I do see the relevance of projects that engage in outlining a particular global journalism ethics (Ward 2005, 2008; Brislin 2004; Seib 2002) to reduce the social tensions in the world, and thereby counteract a possible "clash of civilizations" (Huntington 1993). However, sometimes we tend to forget that the possibility of practicing global journalism radically varies from country to country, from news institution to news institution. One needs to take into account the ideological position of the current news media, the current media system (Josephi 2005; Hallin & Mancini 2004), the ownership conditions (McChesney 2008; Stein & Schejter 2009) as well as various economic, political, social, cultural, etc. barriers to a more "critical global journalism" (Wasserman 2010). See chapter 4.

4. Journalism, including global journalism, is not the embodiment of democracy, as Carey (1996) suggests, but it has an important role to play in a democratic society.

5. Of course, this does not mean that the ethical and critical aspects are neglected, but instead that they are understood in relation to such factors as journalistic epistemology and ingrained news routines. In my view, some negative ethical and ideological aspects of news media might partly be explained as a consequence of the systematic lack of global outlooks in news framing. It is possible to argue that journalism's continuing separation of domestic and foreign news/worlds automatically counteracts a cosmopolitan worldview that could bring "us" and "them" closer. In other words, as a practicing journalist, even if you see yourself as a good cosmopolitan who strives to embrace the entire world, you might still have ingrained "reporting habits" that undermine these well-intentioned cosmopolitan ambitions.

Chapter 2. So What Exactly Is Global Journalism?

1. On philosophical and theoretical discussions of the difference between risks and threats as well as between a risk society and threat society, see, for example, Bostrom (2002) and Nohrstedt (2010).

2. On the other hand, not all financial news services work like Bloomberg's. There is, of course, financial journalism, which includes social dimensions and covers the economy from an everyday life perspective.

3. Intra-global-driven global journalism (i.e., media reporting which is actively "taking part" in a global media process) might generate the need for extra-global-driven global journalism, i.e., coverage endowed with a global outlook. This became the case in, for example, the Mohammad cartoon controversy (2005–2006),

which gradually developed into reporting on a global controversy as it generated political reactions and conflicts across continents.

4. Therefore, one should critically analyze media content, which seems to be very much dominated by mediatization, as the actual mediatization might eventually hide particular political, ideological, or economic interests.

Chapter 3. The Relevance of Global Journalism

1. So, in the push for post-national thinking, we should learn from postmodernism's far-gone critique of modern thought and its tendency to invent "grand narratives" (communism, the market, liberalism, functionalism, etc.) to explain and permeate society in its entirety (Lyotard 1979/1997). As "grand narratives" suppress other modes of thinking, their popularity tends to last for a limited time. Sooner or later they are abandoned and thrown in the garbage as outdated modes of thinking. Let us translate this to the case of globalization: too much globalization thinking in the understanding of society, the future, individual, institutions, etc., sooner or later causes an intellectual backlash. Therefore, somewhat paradoxically, globalization's continuing relevance builds on its inability to explain some phenomena. See also footnote 1 for chapter 5.

2. In this context, one should avoid falling into the trap of historical determinism in the Hegelian sense, that is, to avoid promoting the notion that history is developing through conflicts and contradictions towards an objective idea in which all involved actions, no matter their intention, character or goal, are somehow part of this "objective" process. In this respect, neither global journalism nor any other kind of journalism could be considered to be pre-determined by history as representing the absolute and final stage of journalism. Hegel (1837/1988), Fukuyama (1992) and others are fundamentally wrong about the idea that there could be an "objective" end of history, society, the subject, freedom, democracy, etc., and to transfer this idea to the field of news media and journalism would be more than stupid. See also footnote 1 for chapter 5.

3. Consequently, I argue that this is the case despite the fact that Habermas's study has been deconstructed and criticized from various perspectives (Calhoun 1992; Thompson 1995; Fraser 2007). However, Habermas has helped to explain the rise and development of news, media, and journalism in the Westphalian order, but he has not to the same extent contributed to theory concerning their post-Westphalian destiny (see Habermas 2006).

4. From this point of view, the contemporary global crisis reporting (Cottle 2009a) on climate change, humanitarian catastrophes, forced migrations, etc., could then be seen as highly relevant "pre-mature" examples of a global journalism outside the domain of business news.

5. Despite the emphasis on the observation that the origin of modern news is to be found in the pre-capitalist exchange of market information in particular commer-

cial centers and later on in the (bourgeois) market processes, it is important to remember that economic processes can never by themselves explain and/or predetermine the development of news, media, and journalism. Consequently, one needs to avoid economic determinism, i.e., to see economic relations as the one and only determinant of communicative practices and media (Williams 1980).

6. A potential problem with very spectacular global crisis reporting might be its tendency to reduce the global world into an external "threat" (against "our" territory, traditions, jobs, culture, life styles, language, or environment) (Nohrstedt 2010) in which "tribal" responses (in terms of protectionism, isolation, nationalism), instead of progressive solutions, dominate.

7. It seems quite clear that the crisis of the news media industry tends to lead to overexploitation of extremely safe concepts (Currah 2009). For example, we know that news consumers primarily like to know what happens in the local surroundings, and therefore hyperlocal news (Kurpius et al. 2010) is increasingly expanded.

Chapter 4. Challenges to Global Journalism

1. To some extent, the structuring of challenges is inspired by Fairclough's (1995) three-dimensional description of "communicative events" (Fairclough 1995: 57-62). According to Fairclough, journalism always involves a text (a media coverage, story, piece of news information, etc.). The text, in turn, presupposes discursive practices in terms of inbuilt routines in the context of production and reception/usage. The text and the discursive practices are, in turn, embedded in sociocultural practices, i.e., more general (and ideological) ways of thinking and acting in society.

Chapter 5. Global Journalism and the Digital Web

1. Globalization, viewed as ongoing "writing" (cf. Derrida 1978), has no predetermined essence or mission to fulfill, even though, twenty years ago, Fukuyama (1992), in Hegelian fashion, argued that the (assumed) global victory of Western market liberalism would indicate the end of history. However, poststructuralists as well as most globalization theorists would claim that, in a globalizing world, dominant conditions and powers could always be challenged and/or develop in various directions through the establishment of new relations (of powers, identities, institutions, political alliances, etc.). See also footnotes 1 and 2 for chapter 3.

2. As suggested in chapter 2, some information processes and news flows tend to co-produce globalization. In this context, intra-global-driven journalism refers to news flows and reporting which are active parts and co-producers of a global process. However, in this context, what is of main interest is "extra-global journalism," i.e., how the Web might work as an essential platform and resource for news journalists when representing crises and issues with a global outlook. See also footnote 3 for chapter 2.

3. According to my interpretation, hypertexts and hyperlinking do not somehow originate from the Web but can be seen as fundamental cognition, which is present in language use and communication in general. From the theory of poststructuralism we could learn that speech and writing always involve relations between new texts and existing texts (Poster 1989). Thus, when global outlooks are generated in "old" media (radio, television, newspapers), such as, for example, in the climate reporting in the local press or on television, a hypertextual rationale becomes realized as well.

References

LITERATURE

Adorno, Theodor W., & Horkheimer, Max (1972) *Dialectic of Enlightenment*. New York: Continuum.

Allan, Stuart, & Thorsen, Einar (eds.) (2009) *Citizen Journalism: Global Perspectives*. New York: Peter Lang.

Al-Saqaf, Walid (2010) "Increasing Transparency & Fighting Corruption through ICT: Empowering People & Communities," *Spider ICT4D*, series no 3. Stockholm: Spider.

Altheide, David L. (2002) *Creating Fear: News and the Construction of a Crisis*. New York: Aldine de Gruyter.

Altheide, David L., & Snow, Robert (1979) *Media Logic*. Beverly Hills, CA: Sage.

Althusser, Louis (2001) *Lenin and Philosophy and Other Essays*. New York: Monthly Review Press.

Altmeppen, Klaus-Dieter (2010) "The Gradual Disappearance of Foreign News in German Television: Is There a Future for Global, International, World or Foreign News?" *Journalism Studies* 11(4): 567-576.

Anderson, Benedict (1991) *Imagined Communities: Reflections on the Origin and Spread of Nationalism*. London: Verso.

Augoustinos, Martha, & Walker, Iain (1996) *Social Cognition: An Integrated Introduction*. London, Thousand Oaks, and New Delhi: Sage.

Balnaves, Mark, Donald, Stephanie, & Shoesmith, Brian (2009) *Media Theories & Approaches: A Global Perspective*. New York: Palgrave Macmillan.

Bardoel, Johannes, & Deuze, Mark (2001) "'Network Journalism': Converging Competences of Old and New Media Professionals," *Australian Journalism Review* 23(2): 91-103.

Bardoel, Johannes, & d'Haenens, Leen (2008) "Reinventing Public Service Broadcasting in Europe: Prospects, Promises and Problems," *Media, Culture & Society* 30(3): 337-355.

Barnhurst, Kevin G. (2010) "Technology and the Changing Idea of News: 2001 U.S. Newspaper Content at the Maturity of Internet 1.0," *International Journal of Communication* 4: 1082-1099.

Barnhurst, Kevin G. (2012) "The Form of Online News in the Mainstream US Press, 2001-2010," *Journalism Studies* 13(5-6): 791-800.

Baudrillard, Jean (1982/1997) *In the Shadow of the Silent Majorities*. New York: Semiotext(e).

Bauman, Zygmunt (1995) *Life in Fragments. Essays in Postmodern Morality.* Cambridge, MA: Blackwell Publishers.

Bauman, Zygmunt (2000) *Liquid Modernity.* Cambridge: Polity Press.

Beck, Ulrich (1992) *Risk Society: Towards a New Modernity.* London: Sage.

Beck, Ulrich (2005) *Power in the Global Age.* Cambridge and Malden, MA: Polity Press.

Beck, Ulrich (2006) *Cosmopolitan Vision.* Cambridge and Malden, MA: Polity Press.

Beck, Ulrich (2010) "Climate for Change, or How to Create a Green Modernity?" *Theory, Culture & Society* 27(2-3): 254-266.

Beckett, Charlie (2010) "Quality Journalism in a Networked Age" in von Krogh, T. (ed.) *Journalistisk kvalitet?* [What is quality in journalism?]. Stockholm: Sim(o).

Berger, Guy (2009) "How the Internet Impacts on International News: Exploring Paradoxes of the Most Global Medium in a Time of 'Hyperlocalism,'" *International Communication Gazette* 71(5): 355-371.

Berger, Peter L., & Luckmann, Thomas (1966) *The Social Construction of Reality: A Treatise in the Sociology of Knowledge.* New York: Anchor Books.

Berglez, Peter (1997) "Skrivandets ständiga framåtskridande" [The eternal process of writing], *Rhetorica Scandinavica* 4: 52-60.

Berglez, Peter (1999) "Drömmar och mardrömmar om politiken, massmedierna och medborgarna" [Dreams and nightmares about politics, media and the citizens] in Amnå, E. (ed.): *Politikens medialisering* [The mediatization of politics]. SOU 1999: 126.

Berglez, Peter (2003) "Konsensus, dissensus och objektiva nyheter" [Consent, dissent and objective news] in Berglez, P., Listerman, T., & Mral, B. *Hur Kosovokonflikten kommunicerades* [How the Kosovo conflict was communicated]. Örebro, Sweden: Örebro studier i kommunikation och medier.

Berglez, Peter (2004) "Disconnection: On Mass Media and 11/9" in Nohrstedt, S. A., & Ottosen, R. (eds.): *U.S. and the Others: Global Media Images on 'The War on Terror.'* Gothenburg, Sweden: Nordicom.

Berglez, Peter (2006) *The Materiality of Media Discourse: On Capitalism and Journalistic Modes of Writing.* Örebro, Sweden: Örebro studies in media and communication 4.

Berglez, Peter (2007) "For a Transnational Journalistic Mode of Writing" in Höijer, B. (ed.) *Ideological Horizons in the Media and Among Citizens.* Göteborg University: Nordicom.

Berglez, Peter (2008) "What Is Global Journalism? Theoretical and Empirical Conceptualisations," *Journalism Studies* 9(6): 845-858.

Berglez, Peter (2010) "Var är den globala generationens nyheter" [Where could one find the news of the global generation?], *Newsmill* (www.newsmill.se). March 4, 2010.

Berglez, Peter (2011a) "Inside, Outside, and Beyond Media Logic: Journalistic Creativity in Climate Reporting," *Media, Culture and Society* 33(3): 449-465.

Berglez, Peter (2011b) "Global Journalism: An Emerging News Style and Outline for a Training Programme" in Franklin, B. & Mensing, D. (eds.) *Journalism Education, Training and Employment.* London: Routledge.

Berglez, P. (2012) "News" in Juergensmeyer, M., & Anheier, H. (eds.) *Encyclopedia of Global Studies*. Thousand Oaks, London and New Delhi: Sage.

Berglez, Peter, & Nohrstedt, Stig A. (2009) "Makt" [Power] in Berglez, P., & Olausson, U. (eds.) *Mediesamhället: centrala begrepp* [Media society: Essential concepts]. Lund, Sweden: Studentlitteratur.

Berglez, Peter, & Olausson, Ulrika (2011) "Intentional and Unintentional Transnationalism: Two Political Identities Repressed by National Identity in the News Media," *National Identities* 13(1): 35–49.

Berglez, Peter, Olausson, Ulrika, & Höijer, Birgitta (2009) "Individualization and Nationalization of the Climate Issue" in Boyce, T., & Lewis, T. (eds.) *Climate Change and the Media*. New York: Peter Lang.

Berman, Marshall (1983) *All That Is Solid Melts into Air*. London: Verso.

Billig, Michael (1995) *Banal Nationalism*. London: Sage.

Boltanski, Luc (1999) *Distant Suffering: Morality, Media and Politics*. Cambridge: Cambridge University Press.

Bolter, Jay D., & Grusin, Richard (2000) *Remediation: Understanding New Media*. Cambridge, MA: The MIT Press.

Bostrom, Nick (2002) "Existential Risks: Analyzing Human Extinction Scenarios and Related Hazards," *Journal of Evolution and Technology* 9: 1–33.

Boyd-Barrett, Oliver, & Rantanen, Terhi (eds.) (1998) *The Globalization of News*. London, Thousand Oaks and New Delhi: Sage.

Brislin, Tom (2004) "Empowerment as a Universal Ethic in Global Journalism," *Journal of Mass Media Ethics* 19(2): 130–137.

Buckle, Christopher (2011) "The 'War on Terror' Metaframe in Film and Television." PhD Thesis: University of Glasgow. http://theses.gla.ac.uk/3014

Calhoun, Craig (2007) *Nations Matter: Culture, History, and the Cosmopolitan Dream*. London: Routledge.

Calhoun, Craig (ed.) (1992) *Habermas and the Public Sphere*. London: MIT Press.

Callero, Peter, L. (2008) "The Globalization of the Self: Role and Identity Transformation from Above and Below," *Sociology Compass* 2(6): 1972–1988.

Carey, James (1992) *Communication as Culture: Essays on Media and Society*. New York: Routledge.

Carey, James (1996) "Where Journalism Education Went Wrong" at www.lindadaniele.wordpress.com/2010/08/11/carey-where-journalism-education-went-wrong/ (retrieved August 18, 2010).

Carpenter, Serena (2010) "A Study of Content Diversity in Online Citizen Journalism and Online Newspaper Articles," *New Media & Society* 12(7): 1064–1089.

Carpentier, Nico, & Cammaerts, Bart (2006) "Hegemony, Democracy, Agonism and Journalism: An Interview with Chantal Mouffe," *Journalism Studies* 7(6): 964–975.

Castells, Manuel (1996) *The Information Age: Economy, Society and Culture, Vol. 1: The Rise of the Network Society*. Malden, MA: Blackwell.

Castells, Manuel (2001) *The Internet Galaxy*. Oxford: Oxford University Press.

Chitty, Naren (2000) "A Matrix Model for Framing News Media Reality" in Malek, A., & Kavoori, A.P. (eds.) *The Global Dynamics of News: Studies in International Coverage and News Agenda*. Stamford, CT: Ablex Publishing.

Chouliaraki, Lilie (2004) "Watching 11 September: The Politics of Pity," *Discourse & Society* 15(2–3): 185–198.

Chouliaraki, Lilie (2006) *The Spectatorship of Suffering*. London: Sage Publications.

Clausen, Lisbeth (2004) "Localizing the Global: 'Domestication' Processes in International News Production," *Media, Culture and Society* 26(1): 25–44.

Collins, Richard (2002) *Media and Identity in Contemporary Europe: Consequences of Global Convergence*. Bristol and Portland, OR: Intellect Books.

Collins, Richard (2011) "Content Online and the End of Public Media? The UK, a Canary in the Coal Mine?" *Media, Culture and Society* 33(8): 1202–1219.

Cottle, Simon (2009a) *Global Crisis Reporting: Journalism in the Global Age*. New York: Open University Press.

Cottle, Simon (2009b) "Journalism Studies: Coming of (Global) Age?" *Journalism* 10(3): 309–311.

Cottle, Simon (2009c) "Global Crises in the News: Staging New Wars, Disasters, and Climate Change," *International Journal of Communication* 3: 494–516.

Cottle, Simon (2011) "Taking Global Crises in the News Seriously: Notes from the Dark Side of Globalization," *Global Media and Communication* 7(2): 77–95.

Cottle, Simon (2012) "Journalists Witnessing Disaster," *Journalism Studies* 14(2): 232–248.

Cottle, Simon, & Lester, Libby (2011) (eds.) *Transnational Protests and the Media*. New York: Peter Lang.

Couldry, Nick (2008) "Mediatization or Mediation? Alternative Understandings of the Emergent Space of Digital Storytelling," *New Media and Society* 10(3): 373–391.

Couldry, Nick (2009) "Does 'the Media' Have a Future?" *European Journal of Communication* 24(4): 437–449.

Couldry, Nick, Livingstone, Sonia, & Markham, Tim (2006) "Media Consumption and the Future of Public Connection," LSE Research Online at http://eprints.lse.ac.uk (retrieved September 8, 2010).

Currah, Andrew (2009) *What's Happening to Our News: An Investigation into the Likely Impact of the Digital Revolution on the Economics of News Publishing in the UK*. Oxford: Reuters Institute for the Study of Journalism.

Curran, James, & Park, Myung-Jin (2006) *De-Westernizing Media Studies*. London and New York: Routledge.

Dahlberg, Leif, & Snickars, Pelle (2008) *Berättande i olika medier* [Narration in different media]. Stockholm: Statens Ljud- och Bildarkiv, Mediehistoriskt arkiv 7.

Dahlgren, Peter, & Sparks, Colin (eds.) (1993) *Communication and Citizenship: Journalism and the Public Sphere*. London: Routledge.

Danius, Sara, & Jonsson, Stefan (1993) "Starka tolkningar segrar. Fredric Jameson intervjuas av Sara Danius och Stefan Jonsson" [Strong interpretations win: Fredric Jameson interviewed by Sara Danius and Stefan Jonsson], *Res Publica* 24: 19–44.

de Beer, Arnold S., & Merrill, John C. (eds.) (2008) *Global Journalism: Topical Issues and Media Systems.* Boston and New York: Pearson.

Derrida, Jacques (1978) *Writing and Difference.* London: Routledge and Kegan Paul.

de Saussure, Ferdinand (1974) *Course in General Linguistics.* Fontana: London.

de Sousa Santos, Boaventura (2006) "Globalizations," *Theory, Culture, Society* 23(2–3): 393-399.

Deuze, Mark (2001) "Online Journalism: Modeling the First Generation of News Media on the Web," *First Monday* 6(10): 1–19.

Deuze, Mark (2004) "Journalism Studies Beyond Media: On Ideology and Identity," *Ecquid Novi* 25(2): 275–293.

Deuze, Mark (2006) "Global Journalism Education," *Journalism Studies* 7(1): 19–34.

Deuze, Mark (2007) *Media Work.* Cambridge and Malden, MA: Polity Press.

Deuze, Mark (2008) "Journalism Education in an Era of Globalization," in Löffelholz, M., & Weaver, D. (eds.) with the assistance of A. Schwartz: *Global Journalism Research: Themes, Methods, Findings, Future.* Oxford: Blackwell.

Deuze, Mark (2011) "Media Life," *Media Culture & Society* 33(1): 137-148.

Dewey, John (1927/1954) *The Public and Its Problems.* Athens: Swallow Press and Ohio University Press.

Downie, Leonard Jr., & Schudson, Michael (2009) "The Reconstruction of American Journalism," *Columbia Journalism Review.* Available at http://www.cjr.org/news_meeting/the_reconstruction_of_american_2.php.(retrieved November 9, 2011).

Eide, Elisabeth, Kunelius, Risto, & Phillips, Angela (eds.) (2008) *Transnational Media Events: The Mohammad Cartoons and the Imagined Clash of Civilizations.* Gothenburg, Sweden: Nordicom.

Ekström, Andeas (2010) *Google-koden* [The Google code]. Stockholm: Månpocket.

Ekström, Mats, & Nohrstedt, Stig A. (1996) *Journalistikens etiska problem* [The ethical problems of journalism]. Stockholm: Rabén Prisma/Svenska Journalistförbundet.

Etzo, Sebastiana, & Collender, Guy (2010) "The Mobile Phone 'Revolution' in Africa: Rhetoric or Reality?" *African Affairs* 109(437): 695–668.

Fahy, Declan, O'Brien, Mark, & Poti, Valerio (2010) "From Boom to Bust: A Post-Celtic Tiger Analysis of the Norms, Values and Roles of Irish Financial Journalists," *Irish Communications Review* 12(15): 5–20.

Fairclough, Norman (1995) *Media Discourse.* London and New York: Arnold.

Fairclough, Norman (2006) *Language and Globalization.* London and New York: Routledge.

Falkheimer, Jesper, & Jansson, André (2006) *Geographies of Communication: The Spatial Turn in Media Studies.* Gothenburg, Sweden: Nordicom.

Findahl, Olle (2010) *Svenskarna och Internet* [The Swedes and the Internet]. Stockholm: .se

Foucault, Michel (1984) *Power/Knowledge (Selected Interviews and Other Writings 1972–1977)*. Gordon, C. (ed.). London: Harvester Press.

Franklin, Bob (ed.) (2006) *Local Journalism and Local News: Making the Local News*. London: Routledge.

Franklin, Bob, & Mensing, Donica (eds.) (2011) *Journalism Education, Training and Employment*. London: Routledge.

Fraser, Nancy (2007) "Transnationalizing the Public Sphere. On the Legitimacy and Efficacy of Public Opinion in a Post-Westphalian World." http://eipcp.net/transversal/0605/fraser/en (retrieved February 1, 2011).

Fuchs, Christian (2009) "Information and Communication Technologies and Society: A Contribution to the Critique of the Political Economy of the Internet," *European Journal of Communication* 24(1): 69-87.

Fukuyama, Francis (1992) *The End of History and the Last Man*. Harmondsworth: Penguin.

Furedi, Frank (2002) *Culture of Fear: Risk-Taking and the Morality of Low Expectation*. New York: Continuum.

Galtung, Johan, & Ruge, Mari H. (1965) "The Structure of Foreign News. The Presentation of the Congo, Cuba and Cyprus Crises in Four Norwegian Newspapers," *Journal of Peace Research* 2(1): 64-90.

Gerbner, George (1969) "Toward 'Cultural Indicators': The Analysis of Mass Mediated Public Message Systems" in Allen, W. H. (ed.) *AV Communication Review*, Department of Audiovisual Instruction, Washington DC, 17(2): 137-48.

Gerhards, Jürgen, & Schäfer, Mike, S. (2010) "Is the Internet a Better Public Sphere? Comparing Old and New Media in the USA and Germany," *New Media & Society* 12(1): 143-160.

Giddens, Anthony (1990) *The Consequences of Modernity*. Cambridge and Oxford: Polity Press.

Graf, Heike (2009) "Reflexivitet" [Reflexivity] in Berglez, P., & Olausson, U. (eds.) *Mediesamhället: Centrala begrepp* [Media society: Essential concepts]. Lund, Sweden: Studentlitteratur.

Grafström, Maria (2004) "Ekonomijournalistikens mångfald—en forskningsöversikt [The diversity of economy journalism: A research overview]. Stockholm: SNS.

Grieves, Kevin (2011) "Transnational Journalism Education: Promises and Challenges," *Journalism Studies*, 12(2): 239-254.

Grieves, Kevin (2012) *Journalism Across Boundaries: The Promises and Challenges of Transnational and Transboundary Journalism*. New York: Palgrave.

Gundel, Stephan (2005) "Toward a New Typology of Crises,", *Journal of Contingencies and Crisis Management* 13(3): 106-115.

Guy, Jean-Sébastien (2009) "What Is Global and What Is Local? A Theoretical Discussion Around Globalization," *Parsons Journal for Information Mapping* 1(2): 1-16.

References

Habermas, Jürgen (1991) *The Structural Transformation of the Public Sphere. An Inquiry into a Category of Bourgeois Society*. Oxford: John Wiley and Sons.

Habermas, Jürgen (2001) *The Postnational Constellation*. Cambridge, MA: MIT Press.

Habermas, Jürgen (2006) "Political Communication in Media Society—Does Democracy Still Enjoy an Epistemic Dimension? The Impact of Normative Theory on Empirical Research," ICA Annual Convention 2006, Dresden, Germany.

Hafez, Kai (2007) *The Myth of Media Globalization*. Cambridge: Polity Press.

Hafez, Kai (2009a) "Let's Improve 'Global Journalism'!" *Journalism* 10(3): 329-331.

Hafez, Kai (2009b) "Global Journalism: Myth or Reality. In Search for a Theoretical Base." Paper presented to the ICA Conference, Chicago, May 23, 2009.

Hafez, Kai (2009c) "Global Journalism for Global Governance? Theoretical Visions, Practical Constraints." Speech held at *Power and Pluralism. A Media Seminar on International Reporting*. School of Communication and Design, Kalmar University, Sweden, March 19-20, 2009.

Hafez, Kai (2011) "Global journalism for Global Governance? Theoretical Visions, Practical Constraints," *Journalism* 12(4): 483-496.

Halavais, Alexander (2000) "National Borders on the World Wide Web," *New Media & Society* 2: 7-28.

Hallin, Daniel C., & Mancini, Paolo (2004) *Comparing Media Systems: Three Models of Media and Politics*. Cambridge: Cambridge University Press.

Hamilton, Maxwell J., & Jenner, Eric (2004) "Redefining Foreign Correspondence," *Journalism* 5(3): 301-321.

Handley, Robert L., & Ismail, Amani (2012) "A Watchdog to Reckon with: Delivering WikiLeaks in the Israeli and Australian Press," *Journalism* 34(6): 744-760.

Hanitzsch, Thomas, & Mellado, Claudia (2011) "What Shapes the News around the World? How Journalists in Eighteen Countries Perceive Influences on Their Work," *The International Journal of Press/Politics* 16(3): 404-426.

Hardt, Michael, & Negri, Antonio (2000) *Empire*. Cambridge, MA: Harvard University Press.

Harper, Richard, Rodden, Tom, Rogers, Yvonne, & Sellen, Abigail (2008) *Being Human: Human-Computer Interaction in the Year of 2020*. Cambridge, MA: Microsoft Research.

Harvey, David (1989) *The Condition of Postmodernity*. Cambridge and Oxford: Blackwell.

Harvey, David (1996) *Justice, Nature and the Geography of Difference*. Cambridge, MA and Oxford: Blackwell Publishers.

Harvey, David (2007) *A Brief History of Neoliberalism*. New York: Oxford University Press.

Hegel, Friedrich, G. W. (1837/1988) *Introduction to the 'Philosophy of History': With Selections from the Philosophy of Right*. Cambridge, MA: Hackett Publishing.

Heinrich, Ansgard (2011) *Network Journalism: Journalistic Practice in Interactive Spheres*. New York: Routledge.

Heinrich, Ansgard (2012) "Foreign Reporting in the Sphere of Network Journalism," *Journalism Practice* 6 (5-6): 766-775.

Held, David (1995) *Democracy and the Global Order: From the Modern State to Cosmopolitan Governance*. Cambridge: Polity Press.

Held, David, & McGrew, Anthony (2003) "The Great Globalization Debate: An Introduction" in Held, D., & McGrew, A. (eds.) *The Global Transformations Reader: An Introduction to the Globalization Debate*. Cambridge and Malden, MA: Polity Press.

Henderson, E., David (2009) *Making News in the Digital Era*. New York and Bloomington: iUniverse, Inc.

Herbert, John (2003) *Practicing Global Journalism. Exploring Reporting Issues Worldwide*. Oxford: Focal Press.

Hermida, Alfred (2010) "Twittering the News: The Emergence of Ambient Journalism," *Journalism Practice* 4(3): 297-308.

Hermida, Alfred, Domingo, David, Heinonen, Ari A., Paulussen, Steve, Quandt, Thorsten, Reich, Zvi, Singer, Jane B., & Vujnovic, Marina (2011) "The Active Recipient: Participatory Journalism Through the Lens of the Dewey-Lippmann Debate." Paper presented to the International Symposium on Online Journalism 2011, University of Texas, Austin, April 2011.

Hillis, Ken, Petit, Michael, & Jarrett, Kylie (2013) *Google and the Culture of Search*. New York and London: Routledge.

Hirst, Martin (2011) *News 2.0. Can Journalism Survive the Internet?* Crows Nest, Australia: Allen & Unwin.

Hjarvard, Stig (2001a) "News Media and the Globalization of the Public Sphere" in Hjarvard, S. (ed.) *News in a Globalized Society*. Gothenburg, Sweden: Nordicom.

Hjarvard, Stig (ed.) (2001b) *News in a Globalized Society*. Gothenburg, Sweden: Nordicom.

Hjarvard, Stig (2008) "The Mediatization of Society. A Theory of the Media as Agents of Social and Cultural Change," *Nordicom Review* 29(2): 105-134.

Höijer, Birgitta (2004) "The Discourse of Global Compassion: the Audience and Media Reporting of Human Suffering," *Media, Culture and Society* 26(4): 513-531.

Höijer, Birgitta (ed.) (2007) *Ideological Horizons in Media and Citizen Discourses: Theoretical and Methodological Approaches*. Gothenburg, Sweden: Nordicom.

Huntington, Samuel (1993) "The Clash of Civilizations?" *Foreign Affairs* 72(3): 22-49

Ibold, Hans, & Ireri, Kioko (2012) "The Chimera of International Community: News Narratives of Global Cooperation," *International Journal of Communication* 6: 2337-2358.

Jameson, Fredric (1989) *The Political Unconscious: Narrative as a Socially Symbolic Act*. London: Routledge.

Jameson, Fredric (1991) *Postmodernism or, the Cultural Logic of Late Capitalism*. Durham, NC: Duke University Press.

Jarvis, Jeff (2009) "Let's Build an Ecosystem around Hyperlocal Bloggers," *The Guardian*, 2009-09-14. http://www.guardian.co.uk/media/2009/sep/14/ecosystem-hyperlocal-bloggers. (retrieved October 21, 2011)

Jenkins, Henry (2006) *Convergence Culture—Where Old and New Media Collide*. New York: New York University Press.

Josephi, Beate (2005) "Journalism in the Global Age: Between Normative and Empirical," *Gazette: The International Journal for Communication Studies* 67(6): 575–590.

Karlsson, Mikael, & Strömbäck, Jesper (2010) "Freezing the Flow of Online News: Exploring Approaches to the Study of the Liquidity of Online News," *Journalism Studies* 11(1): 2–19.

Keen, Andrew (2007) *The Cult of the Amateur: How Internet Is Killing Our Culture*. New York: Doubleday.

Kjaer, Peter, & Slaatta, Tore (eds.) (2007) *Mediating Business: The Expansion of Business Journalism*. Copenhagen: Copenhagen Business School.

Klein, Naomi (2008) *Shock Doctrine: The Rise of Disaster Capitalism*. London: Penguin Books.

Kunelius, Risto, & Eide, Elisabeth (2012) "Moment of Hope, Mode of Realism. On the Dynamics of a Transnational Journalistic Field during UN Climate Change Summits," *International Journal of Communication* 6: 266–285.

Kurpius, David, D., Metzgar, Emily, T., & Rowley, Karen, M. (2010) "Sustaining Hyperlocal Media," *Journalism Studies* 11(3): 359–376.

Laclau, Ernesto, & Mouffe, Chantal (1985) *Hegemony and Socialist Strategy*. London: Verso.

Lippmann, Walter (1922/1997) *Public Opinion*. New York: Free Press Paperbacks.

Livingston, Steven, & Asmolov, Gregory (2010) "Networks and the Future of Foreign Affairs Reporting," *Journalism Studies* 11(5): 745–760.

Löffelholz, Martin, Weaver, David (eds.) with the assistance of Andreas Schwartz (2008) *Global Journalism Research: Themes, Methods, Findings, Future*. Oxford: Blackwell.

Lovink, Geert (2010) "MyBrain.net: The Colonization of Real-Time and Other Trends in Web 2.0," *Eurozine* (www.eurozine.com). (retrieved May 29, 2011)

Lyotard, Jean-Francois (1979/1997) *The Postmodern Condition: A Report on Knowledge*. Manchester: Manchester University Press.

Lukács, György (1971) *History and Class Consciousness*. London: Merlin.

Machin, David, & Niblock, Sarah (2010) "The New Breed of Business Journalism for Niche Global News: The Case of Bloomberg," *Journalism Studies* 11(6): 783–798.

Malek, Abbas, & Kavoori, Anandam P. (eds.) (2000) *The Global Dynamics of News: Studies in International Coverage and News Agenda*. Stamford, Connecticut: Ablex Publishing.

McChesney, Robert W. (2008) *The Political Economy of Media: Enduring Issues, Emerging Dilemmas*. New York: Monthly Review Press.

McLuhan, Marshall (2001) *Understanding Media: The Extensions of Man*. London: Routledge.

McLuhan, Marshall, & Powers, Bruce R. (1992) *The Global Village: Transformations in World Life and Media in the 21st Century*. New York and Oxford: Oxford University Press.

McNair, Brian (2000) *Journalism and Democracy. An Evaluation of the Political Public Sphere*. London and New York: Routledge.

McNair, Brian (2005) "The Emerging Chaos of Global News Culture," in Allan, Stuart (ed.) *Journalism: Critical Issues*. Maidenhead: Open University Press.

McPhail, Thomas L. (1987) *Electronic Colonialism: The Future of International Broadcasting and Communication*. Newbury Park: Sage.

McPhail, Thomas L. (2010) *Global Communication: Theories, Stakeholders, and Trends*. Chichester: Wiley-Blackwell.

Metzgar, Emily, T., Kurpius, David, D., & Rowley, Karen, M. (2011) "Defining Hyperlocal Media: Proposing a Framework for Discussion," *New Media & Society* 13(5): 772–787.

Meyrowitz, Joshua (1985) *No Sense of Place: The Impact of Electronic Media on Social Behavior*. New York: Oxford University Press.

Moe, Hallvard (2008) "Between Supra-national Competition and National Culture. Emerging EU Policy and Public Broadcasters' Online Services," in Bondebjerg, I., & Madsen, P. (eds.) *Media, Democracy and European Culture*. Chicago: Intellectual Books/University of Chicago Press.

Morley, David (2000) *Home Territories: Media, Mobility and Identity*. London and New York: Routledge.

Morley, David, & Robins, Kevin (1995) *Spaces of Identity: Global Media, Electronic Landscapes and Cultural Boundaries*. London: Routledge.

Morris, Nancy, & Waisbord, Silvio R. (2001) *Media and Globalization: Why the State Matters*. Lanham, MD: Rowman & Littlefield.

Moscovici, Serge (1996) *The Invention of Society*. Cambridge: Polity Press.

Moscovici, Serge (2001) *Social Representations: Essays in Social Psychology*. New York: New York University Press.

Nederveen Pieterse, Jan (2000) "Globalization North and South: Representations of Uneven Development and the Interaction of Modernities," *Theory, Culture & Society* 17(1): 129–137.

Nelson, Ted (1982) *Literacy Machines*. Sausalito, CA: Mindful Press.

Nohrstedt, Stig A. (ed.) (2010) *Communicating Risks: Towards the Threat Society*. Gothenburg, Sweden: Nordicom.

Nohrstedt, Stig A., & Ottosen, Rune (eds.) (2004) *U.S. and the Others. Global Media Images on "the War on Terror."* Gothenburg, Sweden: Nordicom.

Norris, Pippa (2001) *Digital Divide: Civic Engagement, Information Poverty, and the Internet Worldwide*. Cambridge: Cambridge University Press.

Oblak, Tanja (2005) "The Lack of Interactivity and Hypertextuality in Online Media," *Gazette: The International Journal for Communication Studies* 67(1): 87–106.

Ojala, Maria (2007) *Hope and Worry: Exploring Young People's Values, Emotions, and Behavior regarding Global Environmental Problems*. Örebro, Sweden: Örebro Studies in Psychology 11.

Ojala, Marko (2011) "Mediating Global Imaginary," *Journalism Studies* 12(5): 673–688.

Olausson, Ulrika (2005) *Medborgarskap och globalisering: den diskursiva konstruktionen av politisk identitet* [Citizenship and globalization: The discursive construction of political identity]. Örebro, Sweden: Örebro studies in media and communication 3.

Olausson, Ulrika (2009a) "Identitet" [Identity], in Berglez, P., & Olausson, Ulrika (eds.) *Mediesamhället: Central begrepp* [Media society: Essential concepts]. Lund, Sweden: Studentlitteratur.

Olausson, Ulrika (2009b) "Global Warming—Global Responsibility? Media Frames of Collective Action and Scientific Certainty," *Public Understanding of Science* 18(4): 421–436.

Olausson, Ulrika (2010) "Towards a European Identity? The News Media and the Case of Climate Change," *European Journal of Communication* 25(2): 138–152.

Olausson, Ulrika (2011) "Explaining Global Media: A Discourse Approach," in Pachura, P. (Ed.) *The Systemic Dimension of Globalization*, Available from: http://www.intechopen.com/books/the-systemtic-dimension-of-globalization/explaining-global-media-a-discourse-approach.

Olmstead, Kenny, Mitchell, Amy, & Rosenstiel, Tom (2011) "Navigating News Online: Where People Go, How They Get There and What Lures Them Away." *Pew Research Center*. http://www.journalism.org/analysis_report/navigating_news_online. (retrieved October 21, 2011)

Östman, Johan (2009) *Journalism at the Borders: The Constitution of Nationalist Closure in News Decoding*. Örebro, Sweden: Örebro studies in media and communication 8.

Pantti, Mervi, Wahl-Jorgensen, Karin, & Cottle, Simon (2012) *Disasters and the Media*. New York: Peter Lang.

Parks, H., Robert (2009) *The End of Capitalism: Destructive Forces of an Economy Out of Control*. Amherst: Prometheus Books.

Peters, Chris, & Broersma, Marcel (2013) (eds.) *Rethinking Journalism. Trust and Participation in a Transformed News Landscape*. London and New York: Routledge.

Peters, Chris, & Broersma, Marcel (2013) (eds.) "Introduction" in Peters, C., Broersma, C. (eds.) *Rethinking Journalism. Trust and Participation in a Transformed News Landscape*. London and New York: Routledge.

Peterson, Olof (Ed.) (1987) *Maktbegreppet* [The concept of power]. Stockholm: Carlssons.

Phelan, Sean (2007) "The Discourses of Neoliberal Hegemony: The Case of Irish Republic," *Critical Discourse Studies* 4(1): 29–48.

Phelan, Sean, & Owen, Thomas (2010) "The Paradoxes of Media Globalization: On the Banal 'World' of New Zealand Journalism," *International Journal of Communication* 4: 27–53.

Picard, Robert (2008) "Shifts in Newspaper Advertising Expenditures and Their Implications for the Future of Newspapers," *Journalism Studies* 9(5): 704–16.

Polson, Erika, & Kahle, Shannon (2010) "Limits of National Discourse on a Transnational Phenomenon: A Case Study of Immigration Framing in the BBC Online," *International Communication Gazette* 72(3): 251–268.

Poster, Mark (1989) *Critical Theory and Poststructuralism: In Search of a Context.* Ithaca and London: Cornell University Press.

Rantanen, Terhi (2007) "The Cosmopolitanization of News," *Journalism Studies* 8(6): 843–861.

Rantanen, Terhi (2009) *When News Was New.* Malden and Oxford: Wiley-Blackwell.

Reese, Stephen D. (2001) "Understanding the Global Journalist: A Hierarchy-of-Influences Approach," *Journalism Studies* 2(2): 173–187.

Reese, Stephen D. (2007) "Journalism Research and the Hierarchy of Influences Model: A Global Perspective." *Brazilian Journalism Research* 3(2): 29–42.

Reese, Stephen D. (2008) "Theorizing a Globalized Journalism," in Löffelholz, M., & Weaver, D. (eds.) *Global Journalism Research: Theories, Methods, Findings, Future.* Malden, MA: Blackwell Publishing.

Reese, Stephen D. (2010) "Journalism and Globalization," *Sociology Compass* 4/2: 1–10.

Reich, Zvi (2010) "Measuring the Impact of PR on Published News in Increasingly Fragmented News Environments: A Multifaceted Approach," *Journalism Studies* 11(6): 799–816.

Riegert, Kristina (1998) *"Nationalising" Foreign Conflict.* Stockholm: University of Stockholm.

Riegert, Kristina (2009) "'Same Same but Different': New Twists on Old Problems," *Television New Media* 10: 133–135.

Riegert, Kristina (2011) "Pondering the Future for Foreign News on National Television," *International Journal of Communication* 5(2011): 1567–1585.

Riegert, Kristina, Hellman, Kristina, Robertson, Alexa, & Mral, Brigitte (2010) *Transnational and National Media in Global Crisis: The Indian Ocean Tsunami.* Cresskill, NJ: Hampton Press.

Robertson, Alexa (2010) *Mediated Cosmopolitanism: The World of Television News.* Cambridge: Polity Press.

Roosvall, Anna (2005) *Utrikesjournalistikens antropologi. Nationalitet, etnicitet och kön i svenska tidningar* [The anthropology of foreign correspondence: Nationality, ethnicity and gender in Swedish newspapers] Stockholm: JMK.

Roosvall, Anna, & Salovaara-Moring, Inka (eds.) (2010) *Communicating the Nation: National Topographies of Global Media Landscapes.* Gothenburg, Sweden: Nordicom.

Rosenberg, Justin (2000) *The Follies of Globalisation Theory: Polemical Essays*. London: Verso.

Said, Edward W. (1995) *Orientalism: Western Conceptions of the Orient*. London: Penguin.

Sassen, Saskia (1998) *Globalization and Its Discontents*. New York: The New York Press.

Schlesinger, Philip (1991) *Media, State and Nation. Political Violence and Collective Identities*. London: London, Thousand Oaks and New Delhi: Sage.

Schmidt, Eric (2009) "Inside Google: Eric Schmidt, the Man with All the Answers," *Wired*, issue 08.09. Eric Schmidt interviewed by David Rowan.

Schudson, Michael (2008) "The 'Lippmann-Dewey Debate' and the Invention of Walter Lippmann as an Anti-Democrat 1986–1996," *International Journal of Communication* 2: 1–20.

Schudson, Michael (2013) "Would Journalism Please Hold Still" in Peters, Chris, & Broersma, Marc (eds.) *Rethinking Journalism: Trust and Participation in a Transformed News Landscape*. London and New York: Routledge.

Seib, Philip M. (2002) *The Global Journalist: News as Conscience in a World of Conflict*, Lanham, MD: Rowman & Littlefield.

Sen, Amartya (2007) *Identity and Violence: The Illusion of Destiny*. New York and London: W.W. Norton.

Sennett, Richard (1976) *The Fall of Public Man*. New York and London: W.W. Norton.

Siebert, Fred, Peterson, Theodore, & Schamm, Wilbur (1956) *Four Theories of the Press: The Authoritarian, Libertarian, Social Responsibility and Soviet Communist Concepts of What the Press Should Be and Do*. Urbana: University of Illinois Press.

Slevin, James (2000) *The Internet and Society*. Cambridge: Polity Press.

Smith, Woodruff D. (1984) "The Function of Commercial Centers in the Modernization of European Capitalism: Amsterdam as an Information Exchange in the Seventeenth Century," *The Journal of Economic History* 44(4): 985–1005.

Sosale, Sujatha (2003) "Envisioning a New World Order Through Journalism: Lessons from Recent History," *Journalism* 4(3): 377–392.

Sparks, Colin (2005) "The Problem of Globalization," *Global Media and Communication* 1(20): 20–23.

Sparks, Colin (2007) *Globalization, Development and the Mass Media*. Los Angeles, London, New Delhi and Singapore: Sage Publications.

Spivak, Gayatri (1988) "Can the Subaltern Speak?" in Nelson, C., & Grossberg, L. (eds.) *Marxism and the Interpretation of Culture*. London: Macmillan.

Steensen, Steen (2011) "Oneline Journalism and the Promises of New Technology," *Journalism Studies* 12(3): 311–327.

Stein, Laura, & Schejter, Amit (2009) "Interview with Robert McChesney," *Journal of Communication Inquiry* 33(4): 310–317.

Svensson, Jan (1988) *Kommunikationshistoria: Om kommunikationsmiljön i Sverige under fem sekler* [The history of communication: The communicative environment in Sweden during five centuries]. Lund, Sweden: Studentlitteratur.

Syvertsen, Trine (2003) "Challenges to Public Television in the Era of Convergence and Commercialization," *Television New Media* 4(2): 155–175.

Thompson, John B. (1990) *Ideology and Modern Culture: Critical Social Theory in the Era of Mass Communication*. Stanford: Stanford University Press.

Thompson, John B. (1995) *The Media and Modernity: A Social Theory of the Media*. Cambridge and Oxford: Polity Press.

Thompson, John B. (2000) *Political Scandal: Power and Visibility in the Media Age*. Cambridge: Polity Press.

Thussu, Daya K. (2006) *International Communication: Continuity and Change*. London: Hodder Arnold.

Tveiten, Oddgeir (2006) *Nödvendige nyheter: En studie i journalistikens globalisering*. [Necessary news: A study on the globalization of journalism]. Kristiansand, Norway: IJ-Forlaget.

Tveiten, Oddgeir (2009) "Global Journalism as a Social Force: Teaching Journalism as 'Global Journalism.'" Paper presented to the 19th Nordic Conference for Media and Communication Research, August 13–15, Karlstad, Sweden.

UNESCO (1980) *Many Voices One World: Towards a New More Just and More Efficient World Information and Communication order*. The International Commission for the Study of Communication Problems. New York: UNESCO.

Usher, Nikki (2010) "Goodbye to the News: How Out-of-Work Journalists Assess Enduring News Values and the New Media Landscape," *New Media & Society* 12(6): 911–928.

Utko, Jacek (2009) "Jacek Utko Designs to Save Newspapers," *TED Talks*. http://www.ted.com/talks/jacek_utko_asks_can_design_save_the_newspaper.html. (retrieved November 19, 2012)

Van Dijk, Teun, A. (1988) *News as Discourse*. Hillsdale NJ, Hove and London: L. Erlbaum.

Van Dijk, Teun, A. (1998) *Ideology: A Multidisciplinary Approach*. London, Thousand Oaks and New Delhi: Sage.

Van Ginneken, Jaap (2005) *Global News: A Critical Introduction*. London: Sage.

Vobič, Igor (2011) "Oneline Multimedia News in Print Media: A Lack of Vision in Slovenia," *Journalism* 12(8): 946–962.

Volkmer, Ingrid (1999) *News in the Global Sphere: A Study of CNN and Its Impact on Global Communication*. Luton, UK: Luton University Press.

Volkmer, Ingrid (2008) "Conflict-related Media Events and Cultures of Proximity," *Media, War & Conflict*, 1(1): 90–98.

Waisbord, Silvio (2005) "Five Key Ideas: Coincidences and Challenges in Development Communication," in Hemer, O., & Tufte, T. (eds.) *Media and Glocal Change: Rethinking Communication for Development*. Gothenburg, Sweden: Nordicom and Clasco.

Ward, Stephen J. A. (2005) "Philosophical Foundations for Global Journalism Ethics," *Journal of Mass Media Ethics* 20(1): 3–21.

Ward, Stephen J. A. (2008) "Global Journalism Ethics: Widening the Conceptual Base," *Global Media Journal—Canadian Edition* 1(1): 137–149.

Wasserman, Herman (2010) "Global Journalism Studies 2.0: Beyond Panoramas." Paper for World Journalism Education Congress, Rhodes University, Grahamstown, SA. July 2010.

Wasserman, Herman (2011a) "Global Journalism Studies: Beyond Panoramas," *Communicatio* 37(1): 100–117.

Wasserman, Herman (2011b) "Mobile Phones, Popular Media, and Everyday African Democracy: Transmissions and Transgressions," *Popular Communication: The International Journal of Media and Culture* 9(2): 146–158.

Wayne, Mike (2003) *Marxism and Media Studies: Key Concepts and Contemporary Trends*. London and Sterling, VA: Pluto Press.

Weman, Jon (2012) "Från Kony till Obama" [From Kony to Obama], *Aftonbladet*, November 9, 2012.

Westerståhl, Jörgen (1983) "Objective News Reporting," *Communication Research* 10(3): 403–424.

Whipple, Mark (2005) "The Dewey-Lippmann Debate Today: Communication Distortions, Reflective Agency, and Participatory Democracy," *Sociological Theory* 23(2): 156–178.

Williams, Raymond (1980) *Problems in Materialism and Culture: Selected Essays*. London: Verso and NLB.

Wodak, Ruth, de Cilla, Rudolf, Reisigl, Martin, & Liebhart, Karin (1999) *The Discursive Construction of National Identity*. Edinburgh: Edinburgh University Press.

Yell, Susan (2012) "Natural Disaster News and Communities of Feeling: The Affective Interpellation of Local and Global Publics," *Social Semiotics* 22(4): 409–428.

OTHER SOURCES

Gaghan, Stephen (2005) *Syriana*. Warner Bros Pictures and others.

Gertten, Fredrik (2009) *Bananas!* WG Films and Magic Hour Films ApS.

Moodysson, Lukas (2009) *Mammoth*. Memfis Film, Film i Väst and others

ARTICLES FROM NEWS MEDIA

Chapter 2

"The least guilty—the most punished" [Minst skyldig—mest drabbad] Dagens Nyheter November 29, 2009.

"Nuclear weapons could destroy the world—in 15 minutes" [Kärnvapen kan förinta jorden—på 15 minuter], Aftonbladet March 30, 2010.

"Microsoft's wage: 3 Kronor an hour" [Microsofts lön: 3 kronor i timmen], Aftonbladet April 18, 2010.

"The food that is always on the move" [Maten som alltid rör på sig], Nerikes Allehanda November 29, 2009.

"1 PM: Chat with the Sharifs—live from the Maldives" [13.00 Chatta med familjen Sharif—direkt från Maldiverna], Aftonbladet December 17, 2009.

"Appeal to Privacy to Google" [Vädjan om privatlivet till Google], Svenska Dagbladet (New York TT-Reuters) April 20, 2010.

"H&M's tax i Bangladesh: 585 Kronor" [H&M:s skatt i Bangladesh: 585 kr], Dagens Nyheter June 22, 2010.

Index

Al Jazeera 6, 10, 65, 68, 125
Apple 33, 38, 40, 44
Arab Spring 6, 108
AU (African Union) 13, 44

Baudrillard, Jean 14, 56
Bauman, Zygmunt 35, 74, 82, 94
BBC World 8, 10, 47, 65, 125
Beck, Ulrich 5, 24, 26, 29, 51–55, 58, 67, 108, 131
Bloomberg 5, 34, 65, 69, 71, 100, 132

China 15, 30–31, 42, 48–49, 52
Chouliaraki, Lilie 24–25, 70
citizenship 51
    global 58, 98
    national 13
    transnational 53
CNNi 6, 10, 65, 68
colonialism/colonial 11, 72–73, 96
    electronic colonialism 44, 96
community 58
    business 62
    global 84
    hyper-local 94
    international 8
    local 47, 93
    network 94
    open source 43
cosmopolitan 63
    cities 63
    conversations 68, 109
    ideal/worldview 131–132
    identity 35
    movement through space 69
    politics 43
    reality 55
    sources/voices 109
    subject 90, 116, 132
    world order 53
cosmopolitanism 8, 13
Cottle, Simon xiii, 2, 5, 8–9, 15, 25–26, 29, 38, 43, 46, 57, 60, 65, 67, 70, 73, 131, 133

de Beer, Arnold S. 7, 21, 72, 101, 131
democracy 5, 7, 54, 97, 101, 107, 109, 132–133
    global 13
democratic
    global news flow 71
    infrastructure 96
    legitimacy 109
    national system 53
    participation 96, 104
    political deliberation 13
    public engagement 13, 98
    values 3
Derrida, Jacques 25, 84, 111, 134
de Saussure, Ferdinand 111
determinism
    economic 134
    historical 133
Deuze, Mark 7, 51, 57, 59, 74–75, 82, 92, 101–105, 109, 113
Dewey, John 106–110
Dewey-Lippmann debate 106, 107, 110
dialectics/dialectical 63, 65, 79, 82, 89, 106, 128
digital (see the Web)

education journalism 1, 17, 81, 101–104
    cosmopolitan 102
EU 13, 22, 28, 39, 44, 73, 89, 95, 118

Fairclough, Norman 4, 8, 45, 79, 134
foreign reporting/correspondence 14, 23–24, 28–29, 35, 47, 64, 66, 88, 90–91, 93, 98 (see also global journalism in relation to foreign news)
Foucault, Michel 111, 119
Frankfurt School 106
Fraser, Nancy 51–54, 66–67, 121, 133
Fukuyama, Francis 133–134

global crises and issues (their relations) 43–45
global crises and issues in the media
    climate reporting 1, 11, 84, 126–127, 135
globalization and
    cultural homogenization 4
    post-Westphalian order xvi, 51–57, 60–61, 64–65, 66–67, 76, 106, 133
    Westphalian order xvi, 51–57, 60–61, 64, 66, 76, 78, 83, 133
global journalism and
    cognition/socio-cognition 64, 81–82, 84–85, 87, 97, 135
    epistemology xii, 1, 14–15, 22, 57–58, 72, 97, 108, 132
    glopo culture (global political culture) 13, 29, 51, 67–69, 71–73, 101, 114, 120
    socio-culture 82
global journalism/global outlook and
    cosmopolitan outlook 25–26
    domestic outlook 5, 19, 33, 48–49, 106, 126
    global village 60
    local outlook 19
    national outlook 13–14, 17, 19, 21, 52–53, 55, 57, 62–64, 66, 82–83, 95, 102–103, 105, 123, 126, 131
    various news 47–49
global journalism and global
    capitalism 35, 99
    causes 118, 119
    concreteness 22, 30
    identity 42
    inescapability 22, 26, 28–29
    interconnections xii–xiii, xv–xvi, 4, 35, 53, 85, 88, 91, 122
    interdependence 26, 100
    involvement 22, 24–25, 29, 52
    media conglomerates 5, 35
    network society 5
    north 5, 23, 42, 51, 71–73, 95–96, 98, 100
    power 5, 35, 38–40, 53, 55, 57, 98, 117–119
    south 24, 42, 71–73, 95–96, 98, 100
    space 34, 38, 116–117, 121
    threat xi–xii, 28
    village xv, 5, 9, 28, 55, 60, 71, 77
global journalism and journalistic
    anchoring 87
    distance xv, 25, 38, 45, 88, 117
    domestications (introvert vs. extrovert) 88–89
    ethics xvi, 7–9, 13–15, 25, 61, 88, 104, 132,
    networks 91, 109, 126
    objectification 86–87
    objectivity 13, 15, 71, 81, 97, 101, 106–107
    proximity 36, 41, 47, 88–89
global journalism and the following kinds of journalism
    border-determined 84–85
    border-reflexive 84–85
    citizen xii, 14, 76, 92–93, 108–110, 113
    cosmopolitan 88, 103
    development xvi
    economic global 69–71, 97, 100
    environmental 65
    extra-economic global 69–71, 97–100

Index

human rights xvi
network 109
public xvi
global journalism in relation to news business 11, 17, 34, 51, 62, 64–65, 70–72, 97–98, 100, 126, 133
   cosmopolitan 63
   domestic 11, 40, 46–49, 56, 62, 68–69, 71, 86, 94, 105, 120, 125
   extra-global 22, 44–45, 132, 134
   foreign 9, 11, 22–23, 35, 47–49, 56–57, 66–67, 80, 85–86, 90, 98, 132 (see also foreign correspondence/reporting)
   hyperlocal 59, 80, 93–94, 134
   hypertextual 18, 106, 112–114, 116–119, 121, 135
   intra-global 22, 44–45, 132, 134
   international 8, 11, 60, 66
   local xv, 10, 24, 36, 47, 60, 66–67, 76, 89, 93, 125
   national xv, 18–19, 47, 60–67, 94, 125
   transnational 63
Google 39–40, 48–49, 65, 76–77, 127
   Earth 127
   Search 77, 127
Gore, Al 43

Habermas, Jürgen 51–52, 62, 66, 133
Hafez, Kai 5–6, 9, 21, 67
Harvey, David 52, 54, 67, 71, 100
Hegel, Friedrich G. W. 133–134
Heinrich, Ansgard 49, 76, 91, 105–106, 109, 119
Held, David 4, 52, 58, 67
H&M 41–42, 44, 73

ICTs 5, 35, 39, 42, 96
ideology 15, 43, 52, 81, 89, 97–101, 119
IKEA 42, 56
IMF 69

Jameson, Fredric 4, 56, 65, 71–74, 99, 106, 111

Klein, Naomi 12, 72, 100

Lippmann, Walter 106–110
Löffelholz, Martin 7, 21, 101, 131
Lyotard, Francois 107, 111, 133

MacBride Report 96
Marx, Karl 74
Marxism/marxist 13, 34, 98–99, 100, 110–111
McLuhan, Marshall 28, 116
media
   diversity 95, 109, 113
   logic xvi, 28, 30, 32, 46, 86, 126–127
   pluralism 95, 106–108, 110, 113, 116
   public service 21, 60, 92, 95
   public sphere 6, 14, 62–63, 67–68, 75, 105, 120–121
   technology 4, 5, 76, 106, 117
mediation 45–46
mediatization 22, 45–47, 133
Merrill, John C. 7, 21, 72, 101, 131
Microsoft 10, 30–31, 38–40, 42–43, 72
mobile phones 75, 80, 96, 119, 128
   iPhone 4
modernity 67
   liquid 74, 82
Moscovici, Serge 40, 54, 70, 82, 84, 86–87
multitasking 82

nationalism 13, 43, 83, 126, 134
   methodological 54, 131
network society xi, 3–5, 55, 59, 76, 106, 119, 127
NWICO debate 7

OECD 52, 65, 69, 118–119

Olausson, Ulrika 8, 13, 35, 40, 43, 47, 53–54, 68, 82, 89, 119–120

postmodernist thinking 74, 107, 133
   grand narratives 133
poststructuralism 106, 110–112, 119, 134–135

Rantanen, Terhi 6, 11, 58, 62–66, 83
Reese, Stephen D. 6, 8, 10, 15, 43
Reification 99–100
Reuters 8, 40, 47, 65, 100
Riegert, Kristina 5, 9–10, 36, 88, 120

Schmidt, Eric 39–40, 76–77
Skype 42
social media xii, 18, 28, 40, 45, 59–60, 75–76, 80, 91, 94, 105, 107–110, 113, 116, 118–120, 127–128
   Facebook 40, 77, 107
   Twitter 28, 77, 127
   YouTube 105, 112
socio-cognition 40, 82, 86–87
socio-culture 40, 82, 97, 134
Spotify 42

Thompson, John B. 6, 61–65, 67, 98, 133
Tobin tax 42

UN 38, 121
US 10, 21–22, 28, 38–39, 42, 52, 74, 92, 101–102, 116, 118

van Dijk, Teun 81, 83, 85, 98
van Ginneken, Jaap 8, 14
Volkmer, Ingrid 6, 10, 67, 105

Weaver, David 7, 21, 101, 131
WHO 46

WikiLeaks 44–45, 118
World Bank 13, 69
World Wide Web/digital Web/(Global) Web journalism and 2.0 75, 109 (see also social media)
   architecture 122
   blogosphere 14, 74–75, 77, 92–93, 107, 109
   design 117, 122–123
   hyperlinking 18, 106, 112–116, 118, 120–121, 126–127, 135
   technology 18, 75–76, 97, 105, 108, 128
   UGC 32, 37, 75, 109, 120
WTO 38

Žižek, Slavoj xvii

Simon Cottle, *General Editor*

From climate change to the war on terror, financial meltdowns to forced migrations, pandemics to world poverty, and humanitarian disasters to the denial of human rights, these and other crises represent the dark side of our globalized planet. They are endemic to the contemporary global world and so too are they highly dependent on the world's media.

Each of the specially commissioned books in the *Global Crises and the Media* series examines the media's role, representation, and responsibility in covering major global crises. They show how the media can enter into their constitution, enacting them on the public stage and thereby helping to shape their future trajectory around the world. Each book provides a sophisticated and empirically engaged understanding of the topic in order to invigorate the wider academic study and public debate about the most pressing and historically unprecedented global crises of our time.

For further information about the series and submitting manuscripts, please contact:

>Dr. Simon Cottle
>Cardiff School of Journalism
>Cardiff University, Room 1.28
>The Bute Building, King Edward VII Ave.
>Cardiff CF10 3NB
>United Kingdom
>*CottleS@cardiff.ac.uk*

To order other books in this series, please contact our Customer Service Department at:

>(800) 770-LANG (within the U.S.)
>(212) 647-7706 (outside the U.S.)
>(212) 647-7707 FAX

Or browse online by series at:

>www.peterlang.com

www.ingramcontent.com/pod-product-compliance
Lightning Source LLC
LaVergne TN
LVHW012020060526
838201LV00061B/4389